# BEYOND YOUR WEDDING DAY

## PREPARING FOR A LIFELONG MARRIAGE

**By**

**Jack Quesnell**

**1986, 1987, 1988, 1995**

# BEYOND YOUR WEDDING DAY

## PREPARING FOR A LIFELONG MARRIAGE



Family Visions, Inc.
1400 Homer Road
P.O. Box 30067
Winona, MN 55987



ISBN (0-934835-05-5)

Library of Congress Catalog Number 85-80571

Photographs by Jim Bambenek

Cover design by Peter Walsh

DEDICATED TO

THE ENGAGED CONFERENCE STAFF

# CONTENTS

# *ACKNOWLEDGMENTS*

Numerous colleagues, friends and engaged and married couples have contributed insights, reactions, and suggestions to the development and refinement of this book, yet the special contributions of some must be acknowledged. Father Donald Schmitz, Chancellor of the Winona Diocese, graciously critiqued the overall content of the book and offered assurance of its theological accuracy and doctrinal orthodoxy. John Kippley, Executive Director of the Couple to Couple League and co-author of *The Art of Natural Family Planning,* offered invaluable assistance in the development of the chapters concerned with sexuality, sex and Natural Family Planning. Father Cyril Cartwright, the late Ngaire Walsh of New Zealand, and Father Mark Dosh also contributed significantly to the development of ideas in these chapters. I am grateful for the preface written by Father Al LaLonde, and for the opportunity to contribute to *Our Family*, the magazine which he edits.

Peter Walsh, Director of Family Visions, has not only served as editor and publisher, but as friend, critic and motivator. Sister Ingrid Peterson, O.S.F., of the College of St. Teresa in her role as copy editor and proofreader has patiently read several drafts of the manuscript. Mary Hoke has also helped with proofreading.

I am grateful to Bishop Paul Dudley, Bishop Robert Carlson, Bishop Raymond Lucker, Father Donald Krebs, Father Urban Wagner, Father Wendelyn Vetter, Father David McCauley, Father Donald Kettler, and to Jack and Phyllis Anderson for their help in presenting some of the sensitive issues discussed in the chapter concerning interfaith marriage. I am grateful to Father Francis Kittock and his staff for the way in which the homilies programs and guidance at St. Charles Borromeo Parish have contributed to the overall content of the book.

Mary and Bob Munns assumed almost total responsibility for the content of the "Money Matters...." chapter. Mary has also helped with proofreading. In addition to the contribution, each year they give their time generously to hundreds of engaged couples participating in the Conferences for the Engaged offered at the St. Paul Catholic Youth Center.

Lois Zawislak patiently typed the drafts of the manuscript. I am grateful for her secretarial skills and her loyalty and friendship. My wife, Alice, has assumed a variety of responsibilities that only a loving and deeply committed wife would do. Our daughter, Catherine Mollner, served as an invaluable critic and proofreader.

# *PREFACE*

For some time now, I have been reading Jack Quesnell's work. The consistent message coming through in his writing has always been the beauty of marriage and the blessing each person bestows on the other in marriage. Although Jack Quesnell's views are idealistic, I have never found them to be unrealistic. His work as a marriage counselor has given him a firm grasp on reality. This too shows in his writing, especially when he tries to remind married couples that they carry their treasure in earthen vessels.

Now Jack has written a book to help couples prepare for marriage. He covers all the areas of concern one after the other in a systematic way. The engaged couples are considered as individuals, as members of their families and members of our contemporary society. The thorny question of differences and complementarity is discussed from many points of view. Difficult and delicate questions about premarital chastity, family planning, and interfaith marriage are discussed in an honest, straightforward manner. Underlying everything is the warm acceptance of the Catholic Church's teaching on marriage. This teaching is proclaimed with courage, clarity, and without hesitation.

For most people, the greatest challenge of their lives has been or will be to marry and raise a happy family. This task has taken on formidable dimensions in our day. Couples contemplating marriage need all the help and encouragement they can get. Jack Quesnell's book provides them with a very effective instrument to guide them to eventual success in this endeavor.

It is with genuine love and concern that the author of this book is offering his insight and advice to his readers. For those who accept this book in the spirit in which it is offered, it will be a blessing. May it be a blessing to many.

Fr. Albert LaLonde, O.M.I.

*CHAPTER 1*

# The Challenge of Engagement

Imagine that you are sitting in the bedroom of a couple who has been married for more than 50 years. The husband, who has been suffering from a terminal disease, is talking with his wife who is seated beside him. He reminisces about their courtship, engagement and marriage as he says:

> It started out with you and me, then swiftly
> moved to us and we.
> Proposed that you become my mate, you said
> yes, we set a date.
> Soon vowed to love until we died, it pleased our
> parents and they cried.
> Then two of us became three, we called
> ourselves a family.
> We liked our jobs, they paid the rent, plus for a car
> you had to dent

Well, number four was carried home; our son
had a sister of his own.
We taught them all the Golden Rule, the years
went by, they started school.
Once in a while we would fight, but never last
into the night.
The children grew, they graduated, our
babies even steady dated.
So soon the four became a three (our son had
found a mate, you see).
The years went by and then the three had been
reduced to us and we.
But grandchildren came and we spoiled them
rotten as ours did to us,
We hadn't forgotten.
As time went on your hair turned gray;
as I grew old it fell away.
Eternal youth we couldn't hold, even our
children were growing old.
And now you sit beside my bed, our wedding
vows fresh in my head.
It must have begun with God above, in a few
minutes
I'll thank him for having you as my love.[1]

If you are anticipating marriage and are taking the time to read this book, it is safe to assume that you are serious about your marriage. If that is true, the example of the couple in the poem may help you establish goals for your marriage. They provide a moving portrait of a good marriage. First, they were individuals, and then they evolved to a single identity as a couple. They left the home and life of their parents to establish their own conjugal life and to beget and raise their children. Their children were a witness and reflection of their own love. Although their life was not free of problems and tensions, they were committed to resolve their difficulties and not to let the sun set upon their anger. Through their efforts and because of their cooperation with God's grace, they lived the kind of marriage in which the first thing the husband wanted to do when he met God was to thank Him for the gift of his wife.

Do you want to develop and live the kind of marriage in which the first thing you will want to do, when you come face-to-face with God is to thank Him for the gift of your partner and for the blessed years you were able to live out your marriage on earth? This book will help you review and identify the ways, in cooperation with God's grace, you will be able to live that kind of marriage.

You are invited to begin by considering the references that are frequently made about persons "marrying and living happily ever after," "getting married and raising a family," and "getting married and settling down." Unfortunately, the process of settling down degenerates to a "settling in" which interferes with marital bliss and family stability. While men often gain eight to ten pounds during their first year of marriage, women frequently gain five to eight pounds. You might imagine a husband, after a year or two of marriage sitting around the living room in his favorite outfit—jockey shorts with a hole in his T-shirt for better ventilation. If he receives a telephone call from one of his friends who asks if he is doing anything, the husband may reply, "No, you are not interrupting a thing. I'm just sitting here by myself, no one is here. It's just me and Helen." This woman to whom he had been so very attentive and affectionate has gradually become "nobody."

Of course, his wife may not improve much upon the picture as she sits around in her cutoffs with her hair wrapped up in beer cans as her contribution to the ecology campaign. In fact, the status of a relationship can frequently be predicted by the way in which a couple sits in the car. If a couple drives by with the woman seated on top of the guy giving the impression that she is practicing an emergency escape out of the driver's side, they are probably on their first or second date. In fact, when our sons would ask to use the car with the bench seat, we would usually insist that they use the one with the bucket seats which we refer to as our chastity car.

If another car comes by with the woman seated further to the right, securely strapped in her seat belt, but apparently holding the hand of the man, we may be able to guess that they are engaged. However, if a third car comes by with the woman scooted way over to the right with her back against the door knob, you might safely assume they are married. Although women may want to keep their coats over their shoulders to protect them from the cold, it is a little hard to understand why they want the door knob right in the small of their backs. An engaged couple might picture themselves in this scene two years after marriage.

As they whiz along in silence, they may pass a nostalgic spot which holds many memories from their engagement. As she asks, "Tom, do you remember a couple of years ago when we had such a lovely time in this park?" he may grunt a very conversational, "Soooo." As her heart falls a bit more into her stomach, Patrice may glance at the chasm between the two of them and lament, "My goodness, Tom, look at how far apart we have grown in these two years of marriage." Tom may cast a glance towards the chasm and nonchalantly reply, "Well, it was not me who moved in the first place."

Although engaged couples will agree that their parents, many of their aunts and uncles, and many of their friends have settled in, they frequently protest, "It's not going to happen to us." To insure against this couples should assess the extent to which they may already have settled in to the old age of engagement. One of the common signs of settling in is that couples have trouble thinking. For instance, if one asks the other what he or she would like to do, the response may be:

"I don't care."

"Whatever you want to do."

"Whatever."

"Nothing."

There is a tendency for some individuals to think these responses indicate they are easy going and agreeable. However, they need also to ask how much fun it is to be with someone who doesn't care what he or she does and who does not have any ideas about what he or she would like to do. One husband was patting himself on the back after his wife asked him what he wanted for dinner and he had said anything was all right with him. However, as he was about to throw his shoulder out of joint, he began to realize that it would not be fun to prepare a meal for someone who cared little whether he had hot dogs or roast beef with potatoes, gravy, broccoli with cream sauce, popovers, and fresh apple pie with ice cream. If we keep saying that we don't care, the spouse begins to believe, "You really don't care about me."

As couples settle into the engagement, they seem less willing to put their brains in gear. In fact, it may be helpful for a couple to examine the extent to which their level of activity has decreased with the length of their engagement. During the getting-acquainted phase and for the first weeks after engagement, there is a tendency for couples to be active, innovative and sparkly. They may play tennis or softball, bicycle, canoe, hike or go on picnics. However, as the engagement moves along, they may seem more prone to just sit around. Although that is sometimes appropriate and comfortable, couples often find that their enjoyment of one another is related to the amount of mental and physical energy exerted.

Another sign of settling in revolves around their carelessness about manners. Couples may ask themselves, for example, whether or not they are still thoughtful about holding doors for one another. For instance, a man may be approaching the home of his fiancée just in time to see her struggling up to the door carrying two bags of groceries. As he sees her struggle, he may exclaim, "Betty! That's too much for you to carry! You better make a couple of trips." Are you still concerned about being on time? Have you become a little less concerned about how you are dressed? The virtues of tenderness, kindness and gentleness are extremely important in marriage. The cultivation of good manners develops these virtues. It is important for couples to explore the way they demonstrate:

TENDERNESS
LOVE
CARING

Attentiveness and affection also can be added to these. Attentiveness is not meant to imply a continual fawning and drooling over one another. Instead, it implies a genuine sense of concern and attention to the human needs of each partner. In the same vein, affection does not mean a pawing over each other, but a deep concern for the spiritual, emotional and physical well-being of the other.

After our wedding Mass, Alice and I stood in the back of the church with our wedding party and our parents. As we were waiting for the guests to come out and greet us, my father-in-law turned to shake my hand as he said, "Be nice to each other." I thought, "Stuuupid." I had just graduated from college and thought I knew all there was to know. Also, my father-in-law was fifty-nine years old and I could not imagine what an "old man" would ever know about something as romantic as love and marriage. During these intervening years I have come to realize the serious gaps in my knowledge. I often feel he spent his married life demonstrating how love ought to be lived.

It is sometimes difficult for couples to distinguish between settling in and making the transition from romantic love to a more mature love which prepares couples for marriage. Romantic love is a feeling inside the lover that bells are ringing and a roaring fire is burning inside. A young engaged man once asked if he was really in love. He explained, "It must be love! Whenever I see her, my heart pounds like a trip hammer. What could it be but love?" Although it could have been love, it was also possible that he was having a mild heart attack. Couples are unfair to themselves if they continue to want to have their hearts stormed by love. Rudolph Dreikurs explains:

> Romantic love is a concept hard to give up....We long wistfully to have our souls assaulted and conquered by some mysterious force against which we are powerless. And we are as loathe to relinquish this concept as we were to give up the myths of our childhood. For many of us, the criterion of true love is that it be spiced with a dash of unhappiness, there should be just the right amount of heartache,

> sleeplessness, and inability to concentrate on one's work. Add to this just a grain of jealousy (more would spoil the brew) and one has the secret formula for romantic love.[2]

Although romantic love is sometimes spoken of in a derisive manner, it must be recalled that it is a stage in the dynamic love relationship. A study by Graham B. Spanier is one of the many which suggest that romanticism is not harmful to marriage relationships in particular or the family system in general. However, difficulty is experienced when individuals fail to separate romantic fantasies from the realities of marriage.[3]

Most people could not survive the excitement and exhaustion accompanying romantic love. The temperature of love must simmer down so it can be lived with in both summer and winter. For instance, in the Orient, marriage is compared to putting a kettle of cold water on a hot stove. For the American, marriage is too often like putting a kettle of hot water on a cold stove. This comparison points out the risk of substituting romantic love for the maturity of married love. Couples need to remember the importance of working to develop their love and to reach a gentle and reassuring feeling of comfort with each other. Bernard Steinzor explains, "Love does not spring willy-nilly from good intentions alone as Minerva sprang from the head of Zeus, but human love in all its forms requires painstaking cultivation, concentration, and the pursuit of knowledge—of the self and the other.[4]"

In most instances, it is unnecessary to accentuate the negative side of marriage. A colleague said that whenever he was with a group of engaged couples, he began by explaining that x% of couples are divorced during the first year of marriage, x% after five years, x% after twenty years, and that he thought a couple was lucky to make it beyond that. When asked, "Why are you so negative?" he explained, "Because I want to scare them." The opportunity my wife and I have to be with about 2,500 engaged couples a year has taught us that there is no need to frighten the engaged—they are scared enough! About one-fifth of the engaged couples have friends who have separated or divorced after only a year or two of marriage. And that is to say nothing about the marriage of their parents, brothers, sisters, and other relatives. When the parents are divorced, many engaged couples wonder whether or not each parent will come to the wedding and what will happen if one or the other brings a present spouse or friend. For instance, one woman was terribly upset because she wanted her mother's present husband (with whom she had lived and who had cared for her for many years) to walk down the aisle with her. However, that offended her biological father who would not join in any procession in which "that man" was going to participate.

Because of an almost phobic fear of divorce, it is important to accentuate the positive—i.e., to concentrate on what couples in cooperation with God's grace, can do to develop a truly magnificent marriage. As Christ looked upon marriage as a joyful occasion, today the church looks upon marriage as a solemn sacrament to be celebrated both by the couple vowing themselves to each other for life and by the community of believers. Marriage is not simply a matter between the man and woman vowing themselves, but it is truly a communal occasion. The celebration of the wedding feast at Cana highlights the importance Christ places upon the celebration of the marriage. The miracle of changing water into wine is frequently considered to be Christ's first public miracle. It was at a wedding that He revealed His glory and His disciples believed in him.

Although this does not necessarily suggest that guests need to drink wine at a wedding, it does say that this very holy occasion is to be celebrated. It seems more than a coincidence that Jesus should choose a wedding feast as the occasion to reveal his glory. In Matthew 22:1-10, Jesus tells us, "The reign of God may be likened to a king who gave a wedding banquet for his son." We go on to read that the king dispatched his servants to summon the invited guests to the wedding but that some refused to come. He then invited others. Yet some had excuses for not joining in the celebration. The servants then went out to the byroads and invited anyone they came upon to the wedding. This filled the wedding hall with banqueters. Although there is much to be learned from this Gospel story, the fact that marriage is compared to heaven is a strong indication of the importance Christ places upon marriage. We would do well to spend some time meditating upon the power of the symbolism that compares marriage to Heaven. This is a celebration that is so important that people are to put aside their day-to-day activities and come to witness the vows exchanged by the couple. It is interesting that Christ uses a wedding feast to illustrate the point that absolutely nothing is more important than our salvation. Everything we do is secondary to joining God in heaven.

For the married couple, love is like a rose garden. The potential for beauty exists when the bushes are planted. However, if bouquets of beautiful flowers are to be gathered, the garden must be tenderly and lovingly cared for. Left to itself, the potential beauty will never be realized. It is the same with marital love. If it receives tender loving care, the couple will be able to enjoy the comfort and nurturance gushing forth from a loving marriage. If couples are to open themselves to become truly magnificent lovers, they must be free to celebrate their engagement and their marriage.

---

[1] Father Tim Wozniak, former associate pastor of St. Edward's parish, Bloomington, Minnesota, shared this poem with me in 1974.

[2] Rudolf Driekurs, *The Challenge of Marriage,* New York: Duell, Sloan, and Pearce, 1946, p.13.

[3] Graham B. Spanier, "Romanticism and Marital Adjustment," *Journal of Marriage and the Family,* Vol. 34, No. 3 (August, 1972), pp. 481-487.

[4] Bernard Steinzor, *When Parents Divorce: A New Approach to New Relations,* New York: Pantheon Books, 1969, p.237.

*CHAPTER 2*

# Christian Marriage

Since a large percentage of marriages involves a priest, minister, rabbi or some other person associated with an established church, it is important for couples who are interested in a church wedding to discuss just why they want one. With this in mind consider these three types of church weddings.

1. *Convenience.* In the "convenience" church wedding the couple asks that their marriage be witnessed by an ordained minister to please their parents, or because it hasn't occurred to them that a civil marriage might be less expensive. The couple feels no real commitment to the sacramental meaning of marriage and little desire to enter into a truly spiritual relationship. Engaged couples with this attitude are the ones who become offended when the priest asks them if they attend church, participate in any of the activities, or contribute their time and talent. One man exclaimed, "I haven't been inside a church for seven years. All I want him to do is to witness our marriage, get it over with, and I will never darken his doorstep again!" When couples such as this ask, "Why is the priest hassling

us? All we want him to do is witness our marriage," the most logical response is that, perhaps, the priest does not want to be a hypocrite—to be a part of something that is phony.

2. *Nicey-nice.* In the "nicey-nice" church wedding the party wants to have their marriage witnessed by an ordained minister, but they are not actually aware of the power of this sacrament or covenant. They appreciate the nice altar with its flowers, the acoustics of the building, and the long aisle for the processional. They like the large sanctuary which can hold a truckload of flowers and a large pipe organ booming the wedding march and recessional. If they are to be married in an older church, one of the couple may comment, "Sure we are going to be married at St. Peter's! My great grandmother was married there, my grandmother, my mother—and even my father." Unfortunately, nicey-nice church weddings are entered into by nicey-nice Christians who may tarnish the reputation of other Christians. The nicey-nice Christians enjoy major holidays such as Christmas and Easter. But other than the poinsettias and the Easter lilies, the church needs some perennials—those who are there day after day. It must also be admitted that most of us enter into marriage with a nicey-nice attitude. However, as the grace of the sacrament takes hold, we open ourselves to developing a more sacramental notion of marriage.

3. *Sacramental.* In the truly sacramental marriage the couple is aware of the power of this sacrament and covenant, and they see a church wedding as an opportunity to go to the home of their Father to ask His blessing upon their union. In discussing marriage as a sacrament and covenant, a couple should realize that a covenant differs radically from a contract. A covenant is an unbreakable agreement, such as the one between God and Israel. In spite of Israel's failure to remain faithful to Yahweh, He remained true to them. God uses the story of Hosea and Gomer to reveal His fidelity to His people. This story stands in such radical opposition to contemporary standards that modern couples have trouble relating to it. In spite of Gomer's unfaithfulness, Hosea remains faithful to her. Although he is humiliated in the betrayal, he is willing to forgive. He did this because his marriage was a covenant in which God expected him to remain faithful. This is in contrast to the *quid pro quo* nature

of a contractual marriage which is usually voided when one party violates its terms.

Whereas a contract limits and narrows, a covenant marriage is a partnership of life and love in which there is no "mine" and "thine" and in which the expectations are total. A covenant marriage has God as author, witness, and guarantor. Fr. Paul Palmer points out that of the many words the Romans used for marriage, they preferred *foedus,* covenant. The root meaning of the word is to trust another and to entrust oneself wholly to the other. The idea of fidelity (fides) is rooted in the meaning of covenant.

When Christ established His church, Christians began to look upon marriage as a sacrament. While most Protestant traditions recognize Baptism and the Eucharist as sacraments, the Catholic church recognizes marriage as one of seven sacraments. This does not imply that Protestant churches place any less importance on marriage. It is viewed as a sacred reality because it reflects and symbolizes marriage (or love) of Christ for His church. Since it is based upon and reflects the love of Christ for His church, marriage is a supernatural event where the mutual love expressed is a participation in Christ's love for His church.

The Catholic church views marriage as a symbol of Christ's covenant with His church and a participation in that covenant. Through the grace of Christ, natural love is perfected, the indissoluble unity is strengthened, and the spouses are sanctified. A sacrament is the visible and historical manifestation of God to man. This also implies that the sacrament includes a special grace from God, giving us the power (if we utilize it) to fulfill our mission. Since it symbolizes the redemption and love which Christ brings to His church, Christian marriage is a miniature church in which husband and wife live and sacrifice for each other out of love. Husband and wife are called upon to be to each other what Christ is to each of us. When a marriage is in the Lord, every expression of caring becomes a source of grace.

Couples should discuss the three types of marriage celebrations, identify the kind they plan to enter, and discuss the meaning of a covenant marriage. At the traditional age of marriage, many young people may experience a feeling of rebellion or indifference against the church. Engagement can be an opportunity for individuals to reassess their relationship with God and rebuild this relationship. They may have had some unhappy experiences with the institutional church. Perhaps the wedding can provide an opportunity for a couple to reestablish their relationship with the church. Many couples find it helpful to talk with the clergyman who will witness their wedding about their plans for the wedding as well as about their personal relationship with God. Perhaps, through this relationship, a couple will become sufficiently receptive to God's Word that they will want a truly sacramental marriage. If a couple only desires a "convenience" type church wedding, they should question whether they are compromising the church, the minister, and insulting the believers by going through the motions of a church ceremony. They should also recall the distinction between a legal marriage and the sacrament of matrimony.

The couple who seeks a Christian marriage also may want to consider solemnizing their engagement. This is a ceremony frequently witnessed by the clergyman who will witness the wedding. Along with the intention to marry, the couple solemnly requests that Christ be a part of the engagement. The symbol used at the beginning of each chapter depicts Christ drawing the couple into a deeper union with Him and closer to each other. They are being prepared for the oneness of marriage in which they are united as one in Christ. For Christ will not enter unless He is invited. This fact is symbolized by the picture of Christ standing at the door knocking. As you look closely at the well-known portrait of this scene from Revelations, you see that there is no knob on the outside. Christ can only gain entrance if we open the door. In essence, a couple promises to live their engagement in a way consistent with Christ's teaching, seeking to know if it is His will that they marry. The solemnization underscores engagement as a time of spiritual and intellectual preparation for marriage. Unlike marriage, engagement is not an irrevocable promise to marry. Instead, the couple promises to treat one another with the utmost respect and to marry if they have the ability to resolve differences, and if their love is deep enough. It is a sign of their willingness to let the Spirit guide their decision to marry. Solemnization symbolizes that the couple has supernatural as well as natural powers to meet the challenge to marry and to prepare themselves for marriage. It is very important that each person be free to marry or not to marry. A suggested form for this is at the end of Chapter 13.

It is also essential for couples to make a definite decision to marry. That is, each of them should say, "I want to be married, I want to marry you, and I want to marry you on this particular date." It is unfortunate if engaged couples drift into marriage without each individual making a definite decision to marry. The danger of drifting into marriage is illustrated by those who, some few months or few years after marriage complain, "I never really wanted to marry. You were pushing the idea and I just went along with it or did not have enough nerve to say no."

A sacramental wedding is the best celebration for a Christian marriage. Couples are encouraged to develop the kind of spiritual relationship with God which will cause them to substitute an evening of prayer for a bachelor party. Because of the seriousness of their relationship with Christ, one or two weeks before their wedding, couples, hopefully, will invite their very close friends and family to gather for a special evening of prayer to prepare spiritually for the wedding day and ask for the Lord's blessing on that gloriously blessed day.

Couples who are truly interested in an authentically Christian marriage are, in a sense, rather different and out-of-step in a materialistic society. However, living contrary to cultural standards will not be a totally new experience for those who are considering these ideas and suggestions. The majority of people do not accept the invitation to consider marriage so seriously. In fact, many balk at marriage preparation programs explaining that each person is an individual, what works for one may not work for the other and that they will just have to make their own way. Others may protest that they can learn all they need to know about marriage from their parents, friends, and people at work. One man was being teased because his plans to attend a weekend engaged conference interfered with a fishing trip with his friends. In fact, one friend who was also married suggested that he get a substitute to accompany his fiancée to the weekend conference.

Others who are more passive about their participation in programs explain, "Well, my brother was involved in something a couple of years ago and he said that, when you get right down to it, it isn't all that bad. And when my brother says something is not that bad, on a scale between one and ten, it would rank about nine." People with this attitude will sometimes admit, "Well, I will see what I can get out of it." Although it is important to be open to what one can get out of a marriage preparation program, it is essential to be willing to put something into it. It is a bit like a bank account, the more we are willing to put into it, the more we will get from it.

However, it is interesting to find that a significant percentage of couples enters into marriage preparation programs with extremely positive attitudes. In fact, some seek out programs. Others have noted that they feel sorry for their friends whose priest or minister did not recommend involvement in a program. At the same time, it remains true that many persons are more willing to invest considerable money, time and energy preparing for their *wedding* than for their marriage. As much as those who take Christian engagement seriously may be a bit odd, it is also a bit odd for persons to be ready to live a truly Christian marriage. In fact, those with spiritual attitudes, will generally view the challenges faced in marriage differently than those with secular attitudes.

For instance, I find that when a "seat-mate" on a plane discovers that I am a marriage counselor, I am generally asked whether or not I am married, whether or not I am happily married, how many times I have been happily married, how many children I have, and how they are getting along. Then, it seems that I will inevitably be asked, "What is the most common problem in marriage?" Yet, before I can begin to respond to the question, I am emphatically told that sex, money and communication are the primary problems in marriage. In spite of the critical nature of these issues, couples sell themselves short if they believe these are the primary challenges. If marriage is to be seen more profoundly, the challenges must be seen in a more penetrating manner.

It is important to see communication as much more than just talking. Although these chapters should facilitate and improve communication between partners, marriage is much more than communication. In fact, one separated couple explained, "We cannot understand why we are having such trouble. We are great communicators; we are always talking." It was not long before I realized that, yes, they were always talking, but neither one was ever listening. However, communication involves more than techniques and strategies for persuasive dialogue, assertive conversation, and active listening. Effective communication requires a determined effort to truly understand the other person. It involves an openness to real communication—a common union.

If money were really the most common problem in marriage, most of us would not have to admit to the truth of the law of insatiable needs. That is, as our income increases arithmetically, our expenses increase geometrically. Most of us are able to want endlessly. The satisfaction of one want simply gives birth to two even more intense wants. Engaged couples can explore the truth of this by considering the times that a salary increase, gift or tax refund has rescued them from a financial crisis. However, it is quite likely that if $100 was sufficient to rescue them in February, by April they would have been in need of $200. People with hobbies are good witnesses to the principle of insatiable wants. A camera buff never has just the right equipment. There always seems to be another attachment that could help the seamstress. Skiers never seem to find just the right mountain or thrill to please them.

Engaged couples should discuss their desire for material possessions. It will help to discuss the extent to which they want to begin their marriage with the material possessions that their parents only recently accumulated. If couples do not control their wants, they will never have enough money. To know all there is to know about money management will be of no avail, if couples do not learn to control their wants. Believing that money is the most common problem in marriage, couples think that once they have enough money they will have no problems. Although it would be totally false to imply that people who have the most money have the most problems, most happy spouses will agree that happiness was not achieved by accumulating money. Instead, their happiness may have evolved from the thrill of satisfactorily building their life together.

Alice and I find that some of our warmest and most nostalgic moments revolved around the times we were actively building our life together. After we had lived in our home for about ten years and had made several futile attempts to solve the problem of the water leaking into the basement, we decided that the problem would be solved if we built up the back yard to make more of a grade. On one day, the children helped us haul about 100 yards of black dirt to the back yard. We piled this up about a foot at the back of the house and sloped it off to the middle of the yard. The next day we were laying the sod when I came over to Alice who was dirt from head to foot. Because she is a farm girl, she was in her seventh heaven. I picked her up, and drew her close saying, "You're lovely, you're wonderful, thank you for being my wife and helping us to build a life together. I love you." We often recall that as one of the most romantic moments in our marriage. The landscaping did nothing to solve the water problem, but it drew us closer together.

If sex were really the most common problem in marriage, it would be hard to believe that contemporary couples would have a problem. Instead, those who grew up prior to the mid sixties might be expected to have problems with sex. After all, that was the era in which the guideline for sex education seemed to be, "You don't understand it so shut up!" However, by the mid sixties, the *modus operandi* shifted to, "Well, if we don't understand it, perhaps if we talk about it all the time we will come to understand sex." Now, engaged couples and newlyweds can go out and buy their manual to everlasting bliss in bed. However, by the time they get to page fifty, they find that they need a Ph.D. in gymnastics to complete all the exercises. The reality is that the apparently liberated couples of the contemporary age have sex problems and hang-ups, causing one to think that a couple coming out of the fifties "really had it together."

The problem with viewing sex as a fundamental problem is demonstrated by the husband who complained, "The problem in my marriage is that I don't get enough." When he was asked if he meant that he was not eating well, he grumbled, "No, #*$&%*%*, I don't get enough *#$&*% sex. By $%&*# when I want it, I want it and I want it now." How irreligious to refer to sex as "wanting it" or "getting a little bit" or "piece of." Intercourse involves a total surrender to and acceptance of the other. One does not just "get a little" or "take a little." Marriage symbolizes that one gives himself or herself totally to the other and totally receives the other.

When one husband was asked why he had come to see a marriage counselor, he grumbled, "Because I want to improve my sex life." When he was asked if he was really serious, he explained that he would not pay such ridiculous fees if he wasn't serious about changing his sex life. Then he was advised, "If you really want to improve your sex life, become a saint." At this point, he thought the marriage counselor had gone a bit whacko. He asked, "What in the devil does religion have to do with good sex?" Those who join this man in believing that sex and religion are incompatible have not read the *Song of Songs*. It is perfectly reasonable to expect religion and sex to go together. After all, the closer we are able to unite with God, who is pure Spirit, the closer we will be united to the spirit of the spouse. It is on the spiritual level that couples find the most profound intimacy.

Couples are asked to consider that the underlying and pivotal challenge in marriage does not so much revolve around and depend upon communication as it does upon an openness to a common union, not so much upon money as upon want management, and not so much upon sex as it does upon love. The basic challenge in marriage revolves around becoming magnificent lovers who are totally able to give of themselves and totally able to accept each other.

*CHAPTER 3*

# Discovering Differences

When a couple announces their engagement, they imply several announcements. Couples, for instance, suggest that they have gone beyond the selfishness of the teenage years when their primary emphasis was placed upon the "I" and "me." Now, although the individual remains very important, individual interests, ideas and opinions are not as important as the interests, ideas and opinions that will be developed by them as a couple. During engagement, a couple is challenged to develop a couple identity by focusing upon the "us" and the "we." No longer is it sufficient simply to pursue individual interests, follow individual ideas or to follow just one opinion. Now, the couple must seek to develop a way of thinking and acting together. Accomplishing this reality, of course, implies that a couple will not always agree. In fact, if a couple has never had an argument, one partner must be unnecessary. Rather than to be surprised by differences of opinion, couples should know that differences in background, sexuality, interests, and outlook cause them to look at problems, solutions and challenges of life in different ways. Thus, they should anticipate differences of opinion. Since engagement and marriage are such intimate relationships, it is vital that engaged couples and spouses develop an attitude which is directed towards "working out" versus "fighting out" differences.

One has to face the reality of imperfections. As a result of imperfections, one partner may find it necessary to criticize or offer little suggestions for the other's improvement. Couples must ask themselves if they have learned to offer constructive criticism which, like rain, should be gentle enough to nourish growth without destroying roots. Couples must also ask themselves how they receive criticism. "Am I a Defensive Dennis or Denise who denies all faults?" When we are criticized, we tend to become a Dennis or Denise Yabbitt. All the while criticism is being given, Yabbitts tend to turn off their hearing aids so they can, without undue interference from the facts, prepare their own responses. As soon as the criticizer (who may be a critical Curt or Christine) stops to take a breath, a Yabbitt'er will interject, "Yabbitt..." Then, they say all the things they were busy thinking about while they were not listening.

If couples establish a relationship in which the criticism is gentle enough to nourish growth without destroying roots, they will find that criticism will provide them with opportunities for growth. In the same vein, to overcome an urge to criticize may help to develop a greater degree of tolerance and acceptance. It may be helpful for couples to discuss the ways in which criticism has helped them achieve personal maturity and how the elimination of little irritations has helped them develop a deeper sense of intimacy.

Perhaps criticism may even help us learn to handle our tempers in a more constructive way. For instance, when one of our sons was playing in a junior high basketball tournament, I found it necessary to provide assistance to one of the referees who was giving "poor Timothy" a particularly bad time. When I explained that a pair of glasses might be enormously helpful to him, Alice gently commented, "Shhhh! Don't make a fool of yourself—again!" I dismissed Alice's correction thinking she did not love Tim as much as I did and did not appreciate the need for someone to protect him from a "biased referee."

When the referee made another error, I began to stand and even more loudly to explain the rules to him. This time more forcefully, Alice said, "If you don't sit down and shut up, I am leaving!" Again, I dismissed her criticism, thinking she did not understand sports. When the referee "erred" again, I stood intending in no uncertain terms to correct his judgment. Then as I felt Alice begin to leave, I desperately lunged for her saying, "Please stay, I'll be good." It was not only because she had the keys that it was fortunate that I caught her, but also because she saved me the embarrassment of being kicked out of the gym. Later, I met the referee under different circumstances and he assured me that he had made up his mind that if I opened my mouth again, I would be ejected. Alice's criticism had spared me the terrible embarrassment of being ousted from the gym. From then on, I was a perfect angel at games. In fact, I even became sufficiently sanctimonious so that I suggested other parents "cool it." The elimination or modification of certain irritating habits and mannerisms, like ways in which we eat, how we sleep, how we say certain things may serve as antidotes to alienation and, thus, bring us closer together.

It is also important to consider the way in which we say things and the way in which we disagree. For instance, married and engaged persons should never fight. Rather than fight, they should seek to resolve differences. Fighting implies winning and every time there is a winner, there must also be a loser. Considering that the engaged are becoming one and that the married are to be one, whatever hurts one hurts the other. Thus, it helps to speak gently and tenderly to each other. One way to facilitate this is to eliminate profanity from our vocabularies. Most certainly, couples should never use profanity when speaking to or referring to each other. The gentleness of the language that is to be used may be best exemplified by an author who was being interviewed by a family that had asked him to write a family biography. However, the family explained that Uncle Willy, who had committed murder and died in the electric chair, was the outcast of the family. They wondered how the author could disguise this fact in the biography. The author explained, "Oh, that will be no problem, I will simply say that Uncle Willy occupied a chair of applied electronics at one of our leading government institutions. He was attached to his position by the strongest of ties, and his death came as a true shock."

The idea of differences refers to those situations in which each is right, neither is wrong and yet the engaged couples or spouses are diametrically opposed. Since each is right, it is futile to argue about who is wrong. Instead, it makes much more sense to think of ways in which they can adapt and adjust to each other.

Differences are distinct from problems which evolve from situations in which someone or something is objectively wrong. Change is required if a person is abusing alcohol or drugs, is physically or verbally abusive or has a bad temper. Since differences are much less black and white, it is necessary for the engaged to develop the ability to adapt and adjust. It might even be found that some change in both parties is not a bad idea.

For instance, when a couple begins to explore their different interests, they may begin to see how advisable some change might be. A married couple came to a marriage counselor explaining that their weekends frequently got off to a bad start because one wanted to do one thing and the other wanted to do quite another. The husband had come home on a Friday evening in January complaining that he was tired of being cooped up inside all week. He wanted to grab a quick bite to eat and go cross country skiing. His wife lamented that she had been on the run all week and that she had been looking forward to building a fire, preparing some light snacks and sitting in front of the fireplace eating snacks, sipping sherry and listening to music. It would be helpful for an engaged couple to discuss the alternatives available to this distressed couple. Should they:

Sit home one evening and go out the next?

Go out cross country skiing and then come back and sit in front of the fire?

Go out to a dance where they could be warm, yet do something active?

Flip a coin?

Since couples already have so many activities and responsibilities which take them apart, nothing is solved if the husband goes cross country skiing and the wife sits home by the fire. They should take advantage of opportunities to mesh their interests. Change is indicated to the extent that it is advisable to veer from our self-righteousness and self-satisfaction and to open ourselves to the interests and ways of our partner. In fact, engaged couples can think of how this kind of openness helps them tap their own previously dormant interests and abilities. This openness may lead to a more satisfying life and the development of a more intimate relationship. For instance, shortly after our marriage, I decided to take up tennis. Although Alice had not previously been interested in sports, she began to play tennis. During the first couple of years, she thought it was terribly loving to try to fit into one of my interests. Although I never told her, I thought it was very loving of me to play "bouncy-bounce" with her. At any rate, over the years tennis became one of our most enjoyable types of recreation.

Couples might consider the "HALT" approach as a way to constructively deal with differences. This approach recognizes that at certain times our moods and temperaments demand that we drop the whole subject, agreeing to pick it up later. Each letter represents a particular mood that generally interferes with the resolution of differences:

H - Hungry
A - Angry
L - Lonely
T - Tired

*Hungry.* "H" suggests that some of us find it best not to discuss certain problems on an empty stomach. After eating we may be in a much more conciliatory frame of mind. It is surprising how crabby others become when we are hungry. When our blood sugar level is off, we can become very irritable.

*Angry.* For "A," ask yourselves whether you have ever been angry at your fiancé or fiancée. When you were angry, did you say something you did not mean? If the answer to this is also yes, ask the next question. Try to remember if you knew, at the very moment you were angry that you were saying something you did not mean. Many of us become angry at our partner and say things we don't mean. Although we realize that we don't mean it, it is as though we cannot control ourselves—"the devil made me do it!" At these times we are too angry to be constructive and we should talk about the difficulty later. It is unfortunate that even if we apologize immediately, explaining, "I didn't mean it," an unnecessary hurt is given to the other. Of course, these things must be forgiven.

*Lonely.* If a couple has been separated from each other for a while, it is best to give each other the TLC each needs before discussing sensitive issues. Spouses may find it best to have a re-entry phase. If they have been separated for several days, each has become accustomed to living rather independently. The one at home has developed a certain possessiveness towards the home. Some of the re-entry problems become intensified when a couple has children. The one at home has become accustomed to the children living under his or her flag. Now, when the other parent comes on the scene, the home-bound parent wonders how the partner has the right to an opinion about the way in which the children are being raised. Even though they have been apart for only a week, it is advisable for couples to allow some time to become re-acquainted with each other. For instance, it may be well to agree not to discuss problems or the logistics of living until they have spent their first night back together.

*Tired.* Some people find it ill-advised to discuss controversial issues when they are tired. Although St. Paul warns the Ephesians that we should not let the sun set upon our anger, some of us fear that if we do not, we will be up all night fighting. Some people find they become terribly sensitive and "bleed" very easily when fatigued. Some of us become so thin skinned that we could sit on a dime and tell if it is heads or tails. For instance, I returned late one Sunday evening from a busy weekend retreat. I had looked forward to relaxing and talking with Alice. Unfortunately, we made the mistake of talking about a very difficult issue. We were doing some remodeling of our home and we began talking about where the materials should be stored. To have my suggestion rejected regarding the storage of building materials was the "deepest hurt" I could imagine. Fortunately, as the discussion became heated, Alice had the presence of mind to exclaim, "HALT!" We were too tired and lonely to discuss something so "sensitive and important." Some eight hours later neither of us really cared where the materials were piled. On the previous evening, we each needed TLC and not a discussion about remodeling.

One couple, who had been married for fifty years, explained that the most helpful recommendation the priest made to them before marriage was not to let the sun set upon their anger. If couples discipline themselves to kneel each evening to thank God for His blessings and to ask for forgiveness, the tensions, and hurts that divide them will be reconciled. It is very hard to remain on the offensive or defensive when you are side-by-side before the all-loving God. Try to integrate this scriptural ideal into your lives.

## *CHAPTER 4*

# Sexual Differences

When confronted by those situations in which someone or something is wrong, change is required. While problems require change, differences require adaptation and adjustment. It is not always simple to identify whether one is dealing with a difference (requiring adaptation) or a problem (requiring change). For instance, one partner may complain that the other is abusing alcohol. The "accused partner" may protest that the other comes from a family background in which alcohol was held as taboo. Thus a friendly or social drink is objected to and looked upon as an abuse. What one partner considers a social nicety is looked upon by the other as a vice.

Temper or emotions frequently challenge couples to distinguish between a problem or a difference. Although many persons acknowledge their bad tempers, they generally blame it on their genetic composition. They argue, for example, that a bad temper is characteristic of the French, German, or Irish. However, almost every national group is known for its bad temper. A bad temper might be the individual's make-up and not something for which he or she should blame ancestors. Yet is the matter of temper and emotionality really a problem requiring change or a difference requiring adaptation and adjustment?

When one partner comes from an extremely placid home and the other from a more expressive home, they frequently end up in a charger vs. retreater relationship. The charger is committed to working out and dissolving tension. He or she may charge forth exclaiming that they cannot sit in their own corners licking their wounds, "WE HAVE GOT TO GET THIS SETTLED!"

The other partner may retreat thinking, "We are saying hurtful things, we are raising our voices, it is best to stay away from each other for awhile." Peaceful Percy or Priscilla interprets the raised voice and excited gestures as unloving signs. However, the more rambunctious of the two thinks it is very unloving to retreat into silence. As spouses, the charger turns into a nocturnal churner. If the sun has set upon their anger, the stomach of the charger is churning, his thoughts are racing and it is impossible to sleep. He turns over exclaiming, "We can't go to sleep like this. We have got to talk about it. Let's get this worked out!" The only sound heard from the other is zzzzzzz.

Of course, the sound of the snoring really sets the charger to churning. His stomach becomes a veritable roller coaster as he laments, "She doesn't care, she doesn't love me, what's the use? How can anyone sleep when it's so tense between us?" However, the charger fails to understand the reasoning of the snorer. The snorer simply thinks that, at least, if we are sleeping, we will not hurt each other and things may seem a lot different in the morning.

One partner may come from a placid and tranquil family such as the wife who explained that, in all her fifty years, she had had only one argument with her parents. This occurred when she was fifteen years old and was late returning to the car during a trip the family had taken into town. Her father asked, "Where have you been?" She replied, "Well! I am only fifteen minutes late!" Later in her adult life, she lamented that that was the only time her father had ever spoken harshly to her. She regretted that, on this one occasion, she had sassed her parents. Her father had replied, "Get into the car, you are not yet dry behind the ears!" She always felt bad that her father had found it necessary to scold her.

Another man explained that his father was a patient man who operated on the premise that his children never made mistakes—there were just things they had to do over. During the boy's teenage years, his father traded their two-row corn picker for a six-row picker. The price tag had not come off the new picker before the boy ran it into a bridge pillar. The father, looking at the battered corn picker, said, "Well, it is going to take a lot longer with the two row-picker." Someone growing up in such a peaceful environment may have difficulty with a spouse who tends to be more volatile and explosive.

Some of the differences are expressed in funny little ways such as the time in early December when Alice mentioned that she needed a pair of earmuffs. I asked, "Do you want to pick them up or do you want me to stop to get them for you?" Alice replied that that was a hint for a Christmas present. I said, "My word, if you want a pair of earmuffs, get a pair of earmuffs and don't wait until Christmas." To this Alice replied, "That's the trouble with you. Whenever you want something, you get it, and then there's nothing to get you for Christmas." I replied that Christmas gifts were supposed to be something out of the ordinary, and not something you would get for yourself. If a couple is going to argue about who is right about such questions, they will not be in any mood to celebrate Christmas.

In many respects, our sexuality provides us with some idea of the need for adaptation and adjustment. At least 95% of those entering into marriage would rank sexual differences as the primary factor in mate selection. That is, about 95% of us would only marry someone of the opposite sex. Yet many people do not consider why they have such a strong investment in marrying someone of the opposite sex. Although it may sound a little crass, the explanation is as simple as looking at a male and female and recognizing that they were made to fit. In fact, as engaged couples are holding each other, one or the other may comment, "We fit so well." Anyone with a basic awareness of plumbing and electricity realizes that the primary fittings are referred to as male and female. Once, when I was "pretzeled" under the sink trying to do some repairs, I asked my daughter to hand me a female fitting. She said, "Oh, Dad, you gross me out, there must be another name."

The sexual differences are intended to be complementary—to bring about a fit. This physical complementarity should mirror a deeper emotional and spiritual fit. The sexual complementarity is the same type we would want to achieve from the differences in our backgrounds. It is unfortunate that differences are sometimes viewed as deficiencies, rather than as signs of our interdependency and as challenges to create a fit. There are some experts who maintain that the concept of sexual differences is responsible for child abuse. They believe that talk about sexual differences suggests a hierarchy in which the male is superior and the female is inferior. Thus, if we are to do something about child abuse, they believe we must destroy the "myth" that there are differences between males and females.

Although the fact of sexual differences influences the roles and functions we play in building up the community of God, the differences do not imply inequality. We are different persons of immeasurable worth. The denial of sexual differences is a sign of the colossal pride afflicting humankind and implies that people will write their own rules rather than seek to understand God's intention. This denial suggests that persons are sufficient unto themselves and, as such, we deny our dependence upon God and our interdependent relationships with others. In an earlier age, marriage educators described the wife as the heart of the home and the husband as the head of the home. This was a symbolic way of saying that a woman brought love and warmth to the home while the father physically supported the family and contributed to a sense of order. Each performed his or her role for the fulfillment of the entire family. Unfortunately, as this symbolism became distorted and misunderstood, the entire teaching was disregarded.

Many discussions of the intrinsic differences between the sexes become volatile and follow the path of the drunk going down the road and only crossing the center of the line as he veers from one ditch to the other. Some misplaced emphases of the 1950's had the effect of enslaving some men and women to distorted ideas about the roles of men and women. So much emphasis was placed upon men being strong and unemotional that some seemed to be unaware of the need to be warm, kind and tender. Because women were expected to be emotional, some forgot that they also had the capacity to be calm, cool and collected. By the mid-sixties, both valid and invalid ideas about sexual characteristics were being sloughed off. A Christian appreciation of the immeasurable worth of both a man and woman entails a recognition of differences and a realization of talents, responsibilities, gifts possessed, and the related contribution expected. It implies a recognition of how people are to serve others, that they are not to be imprisoned by invalid stereotypes and that they can be different without being inferior.

Rather than deny the reality of the differences, we must explore the ways differences help us create a fit—a oneness. The fact that we are male or female—sexual beings—is one of the most obvious facts about us. In fact, the joyful proclamation, "It's a boy!" or "It's a girl!" is the usual way in which births are announced. A histologist can examine a sample of tissue taken from any part of the body and identify whether the sample came from the body of a man or a woman. A piece of skin or a scraping from the inside of the cheek of the mouth can be identified as coming from the body of a male or female.

Sexuality is more than a biological accident or a quirk of fate. It is a mystery, not in the sense of a detective story, but a truth revealed to Christians through the Spirit. A mystery discloses truth about the very inner life of God, His love for humankind, and how He both nurtures and protects life. Since God reveals part of Himself through our sexuality, those who develop a deeper love for God will also develop a deeper understanding of their masculinity or femininity. C. S. Lewis, in *The Four Loves* , recognizes this. "God has impressed some sort of likeness to Himself in all that He has made." Realizing that God is love, a person can also appreciate that the mystery of sexuality is understood only within the context of friendship and love.

In a small way, the conception of a child by a loving father and mother parallels the life of God in the mystery of the Blessed Trinity. In the one Divine Nature of God there are three distinct persons. The first person knows himself, and his active knowing produces an Idea, a Word. And this Idea, this Word—the perfect image of himself—is the second person. St. John writes, "In the beginning was the Word..." The first and second person combine in an act of love—the love of one another, love of the Godhead which is their own, and this act of loving produces a state of lovingness within the Divine Nature. Into this lovingness, Father and Son pour all they have and all they are without holding back. This lovingness within the Godhead is absolutely equal to the Father and the Son for they have poured their all into it. Their infinite eternal loving is another person—the Holy Spirit—the third person of the Trinity. The love between the Father and the Son is so powerful, so real and full of life that it becomes the very being of the Holy Spirit.

Through God's gift of human sexuality, men and women enter into a profound spiritual, emotional, and physical union that is life-giving. As the Spirit is a sign of God's love, a child is a sign of the profound love of a couple. Although children may also be born of unions lacking this love, the imperfect use of human sexuality does not subtract from the divine model. Thus a man, made in God's image, gives love to a woman, made in God's image, who receives and returns his love and their love becomes a child who is a distinct third person.

## Persons of Immeasurable Worth

Men and women are persons of immeasurable worth. Isaiah emphasizes this in writing, "Because you are precious in my eyes and glorious, and because I love you, I give men in return for you and people in exchange for your life (Isaiah 43:4)." On the one level, our equality is a given: we are equal in human worth and dignity before God. However, on another level, we are not actually equal, so we must be very careful not to drive the equality issue into the ground. Simply because some persons are more intelligent, economically wealthy, physically strong, or physically coordinated, does not deny the fact of our immeasurable worth. The unborn child, the newborn child, the mentally retarded, the emotionally handicapped, the developmentally disabled, the young, and the old are all very different and do not have equal opportunities available to them. Yet, they are equal in that they are created by God, are precious in His sight, and therefore, are persons of immeasurable worth. However, if we base equality on some sort of statistical average, there is the danger of devaluing those who do not measure up to the norm. An engaged couple's love relationship will grow if they remember the overwhelming fact of their immeasurable worth and that each of them is so important that Christ has died for them.

The life of Maximilian Kolbe illustrates his belief in the immeasurable worth of each person. In 1951, I sat in an eighth grade classroom as Sister Bernadine told us the story of Maximilian Kolbe. It is the profound love story of a man who gave his life so that another might live. He was imprisoned in a Nazi concentration camp on February 17, 1941. Eventually, he ended up in Auschwitz. Throughout his imprisonment, he consoled and comforted the other prisoners. Despite strict orders against religious practices, Father Kolbe heard confessions, gave spiritual counsel, and encouraged perseverance saying, "Confide in the Immaculate Mother and she will help you to endure all." The year 1941 had been especially disastrous for the inmates of the concentration camps. These death chambers of the German Third Reich were cruel, and the most inhuman treatment was inflicted on the prisoners. For one escapee, a dozen or so prisoners would be condemned to a death sentence. At the close of July, 1941, one of the prisoners escaped from Father Kolbe's Block 14. As a punishment, Commandant Fritsch condemned ten prisoners to death by starvation.

Suddenly, among the condemned, a sob broke out. "Oh God, my wife and my children!" Then something unheard of happened. One prisoner stepped forward and walked toward the commandant. Fritsch, grabbing his revolver, shouted, "What does this swinish beast want?"

Kolbe replied, "I want to die in place of one of the condemned. When Fritsch asked him, "Why?" Kolbe simply responded, "I am a single man, and he (pointing to the weeping Franciszek Gajowniczek) has a wife and children." When Fritsch asked his profession, Kolbe simply replied, "A Catholic priest." Father Kolbe had publicly professed his faith and the love of Christ. "Greater love than this no one has, than to lay down his life for his friends (John 15:13)."

Father Kolbe was taken to the starvation bunker in place of Franciszek Gajowniczek. The fact that Father Kolbe would sacrifice his life for the father of a family stirred the entire camp. The Germans were struck dumb. The fellow prisoners wondered, "Is it possible for one to give up, not just a slice of bread or a few spoons of soup, but his life to save the life of a father of a family?" At that moment, in the splendor of Father Kolbe's heroic sacrifice, a vision of a new and better life presented itself to the prisoners. Completely naked, the ten condemned men were shoved into their death cell, and once and for all the door was slammed behind them. Without food or a drop of water, they awaited their inevitable death.[5]

Father began praying aloud while others joined in. "We fly to your patronage, O Holy Mother of God...Holy Mother of God, do not abandon us in the hour of our death." The echo of his prayers traveled into the cells of other prisoners, and the place of torment and despair was transformed into a chapel of praying men. The days passed slowly as the prisoners died one by one. Father Kolbe's eyes were so clear and penetrating that the SS-men were unable to stand their brightness. They shouted, "Look at the ground, not at us!" One of the soldiers acknowledged, "A cleric like this one we have never seen; he must be an unusual person." To the SS-men, Father Kolbe's agony was too prolonged. Since they needed the cells for other condemned prisoners, they decided to hasten the end of the remaining survivors. On August 14, the camp executioner, Boch, killed Father Kolbe and the remaining prisoners with an injection of carbolic acid.

As Sister Bernadine told us this story, I thought, "I would sure hate to be Franciszek Gajowniczek." During the next thirty years, I read more about Father Kolbe and heard more references to him. Each time I was reminded of Father Kolbe, I thought Franciszek Gajowniczek must experience a terrible sense of responsibility to do something good with his life—to make it worthwhile for Father Kolbe to have died for him. Finally, by the time of Maximilian's canonization on October 10, 1982, for which Franciszek Gajowniczek was present, I realized that each of us faces the same responsibility which faced Franciszek Gajowniczek. We are people of such immeasurable worth that someone—Jesus Christ—died for each and every one of us. Engaged couples should remember that they are engaged to a person of such unfathomable beauty and inherent worth that Christ died for that person.

As people of immeasurable worth, men and women have been created with intrinsic differences which are complementary. God insured our immeasurable worth when he said, "Let us make man in our image, after our likeness." Referring to both male and female, God said, "They are to have dominion over all else on the earth."

In the same way that genital differences have a complementary effect which enable man and woman to enter into a union, the various other differences can bring about a fit, a oneness, a completeness. A necessary step in Christian maturation, engagement and marriage is the acceptance of self as either male or female. Male and female traits go beyond cultural customs and are biologically influenced, but not determined. Although there is still much to understand about the influence male and female hormones have upon behavior, roles, and functions, it is generally agreed that we are emotionally and physically affected by hormones. Since testosterone is a dominant hormone surging through men, and estrogen through women, we can expect that men and women will have different physical traits and capabilities and different emotional responses. The challenge of the physical and behavioral sciences has been to identify the scope and exact nature of the impact of the hormonal difference. For instance, it is agreed that estrogen helps effect the rounding of the breasts and buttocks and the narrowing of the waist. During the middle years, its decline contributes to sagging breasts and buttocks and disappearance of a waistline.

Since physical and emotional characteristics are influenced by sexual gender, men and women should work in harmony with their sexuality avoiding the extremes of either the biological determinist who claims that all behavior is determined, or the cultural determinist who claims that all behavior is learned through cultural emphases, bias and teaching. The truth is found through an understanding of the influences of culture, biology, God's plan, and the unique God-given gifts possessed by each individual. The affirmation of self involves saying "yes" to our bodily and emotional characteristics.

Unfortunate references to "the Battle Between the Sexes" promote greater misunderstanding of sexuality. They hamper the realization that complementary differences between the sexes are to be understood within a loving relationship such as that between child and parent, husband and wife, spiritual advisor and advisee or confessor and penitent.

## Sexuality, Hormones and Fertility

Misunderstanding and/or misinformed men frequently complain, "Yeah, you can't depend upon a woman. She is always changing her mind." Rather than to exaggerate this complaint, the person who understands a woman's menstrual cycle, realizes that mood changes are to be expected. A woman's menstrual cycle, which is controlled by hormonal activity, affects her outlook, psychology, and her total approach to life. A man, not having the same sort of cycle, tends to be more predictable. A review of the menstrual cycle can lead to an understanding of why it has such a strong influence upon a woman.

In early adolescence, girls notice a spotting of blood from the vagina which signals the beginning of menstruation. During each cycle the uterus is prepared for conception when its lining thickens and fills with blood and prepares for the possible implantation of a "little one." If fertilization does not occur, about twelve to sixteen days after ovulation, the lining, along with some blood, sloughs off, flows through the cervix and vagina, and out of the body in what is referred to as the period or menstruation. This usually lasts three to five days. During the first several years, the menstrual cycle is very irregular. As the woman matures, her cycle becomes more regular with ovulation occurring about once every month. When she enters menopause, it again becomes irregular and finally ceases.[6] Menstruation announces the transition from girlhood to young womanhood. John and Nancy Ball describe this beautifully by comparing the menstrual cycle to the seasons of the year.[7]

The menstrual cycle is influenced by hormones which are glandular secretions that affect the other bodily organs. Early in the menstrual-fertility cycle, the pituitary gland located near the base of the brain secretes a hormone called the follicle stimulating hormone (FSH) which affects follicles in the ovaries. Under the influence of the FSH, an ovarian follicle secretes estrogen which causes the inner lining of the uterus (the endometrium) to build up. After about a week, the pituitary gland sends out a big surge of another hormone, LH (luteunizing hormone) and the combination of the high estrogen level and the LH surge causes ovulation to occur. The ovum or egg is released from the ovary and begins its passage through one of the fallopian tubes to the uterus.

After ovulation, the same follicle that was producing the pre-ovulation estrogen gets a new look, a new name, and a new function. It turns yellowish and is called *corpus luteum,* which means "yellow body." It secretes the second basic female hormone, progesterone, for the rest of the cycle. If pregnancy has not occurred, progesterone is secreted for about two weeks, maintaining the endometrium with a rich blood supply. Then the corpus luteum ceases the production of progesterone, the endometrium is no longer sustained, and it is sloughed off in the process of menstruation.

The high levels of progesterone inhibit further ovulations during that cycle. Once the progesterone level has dropped and menstruation occurs, the pituitary swings into action, starting the whole cycle over again. This cyclical process changes a woman's hormonal pattern each cycle so that estrogen is dominant before ovulation and progesterone is dominant after ovulation. This rhythm is why John and Nancy Ball describe a woman as cyclical in makeup.

The menstrual cycle is also the fertility cycle. Rising levels of estrogen before ovulation cause the cervix (the lower part of the uterus that protrudes into the vagina) to secrete a mucus which, close to ovulation, becomes quite clear and stretchy. Also, the tip of the cervix softens and the mouth of the cervix opens slightly. After ovulation, the higher levels of progesterone and the reduced level of estrogen cause the mucus to disappear and the cervix to become firm and closed again. In addition, the progesterone causes a woman's waking temperature to rise about one-half of one degree Fahrenheit.

Sperm life during the fertile time normally ranges from two to five days, and the ovum lives only for eighteen to twenty-four hours. The combined lives of sperm and ovum determine that if a husband and wife abstain from intercourse several days prior to ovulation (to allow for the life of the sperm) and a few days after ovulation (to allow for the life of the ovum), they will not conceive a child. Through an awareness of Natural Family Planning, husbands and wives are able to cooperate with God to either achieve or postpone pregnancy.

Another sign of ovulation experienced by some women is called inter-menstrual pain (or ovulation pain or *mittelschmerz*). If a young woman or her parents are unaware of this sign of ovulation, they may become alarmed when she complains about a pain in her side. Sometimes this pain is confused with the symptoms of an appendicitis attack. A couple of visits to the doctor may help a young woman distinguish between an appendicitis attack and inter-menstrual pain. As ovulation occurs, the ovum is expelled from the ovary. A woman may experience some ovulatory pain as the ovum breaks through a thin membrane that covers its follicle container. This pain may last a few hours or a couple days. Whether the pain occurs on the left or right side depends upon which ovary is releasing the ovum. Other explanations are that the pain may be due to tubal spasm or to tubal congestion of mucus.

There are various other signs of fertility which are unique to particular women. For instance, if a young woman becomes aware of her signs of fertility, she may notice that because of the hormonal activity her hair may become more oily or that she may have more difficulty with acne at some times than at others.

An understanding of the fertility cycle leads to an understanding of the pre-menstrual syndrome which involves a constellation of physical and emotional symptoms. Towards the end of the pre-menstrual cycle, a woman may seem less able to cope with life, finding that she is less careful and less attentive. A perceptive student may prefer to take her examinations during the earlier phase of her cycle, but instructors obviously would have difficulty scheduling exams around every woman's cycle. Unfortunately, men have frequently placed inordinate emphasis upon this phase of the cycle when a woman is sometimes less happy and more tense. We notice less frequently the mid-cycle mood when the estrogen is rising rapidly and many women have a greater feeling of well-being. At mid-cycle, many women are more energetic and active; they make decisions more quickly and definitely.

There is some speculation that a particular scent is emitted around the time of ovulation (fertility). This, along with a particular glow, may make a husband more aware of his wife's presence. The way in which a wife kisses her husband may telegraph the fact that she is ovulating. As a result of practicing Natural Family Planning, spouses become very aware of the moods associated with various phases of the cycle. Thus, after gaining some experience, spouses may crosscheck the mood of the wife with the fertility chart. As one husband kissed his wife, he commented, "Ohhh, you're ovulating today." The somewhat startled wife asked, "How can you tell?" Of course, her very special warmth and closeness gave him the message.

This realization can help the engaged couple to reserve the gift of intercourse for marriage. As the woman approaches ovulation and while she is ovulating, it may be more difficult for her to adhere to their commitment to chastity. During these times, a woman needs a very loving man who will revere the sacredness of chastity and tenderly help them adhere to their commitment to reserve intercourse for marriage. As John and Nancy Ball point out, "Our hope for the future is that each young woman may learn to accept and to live with the seasons of her cycle. If she enters into a conjugal commitment, this hope can only be fulfilled if she marries a 'man for all seasons.'"[8]

Chastity helps partners learn to live creatively and positively with fertility rather than to curse it as a disease. The more a couple learns to understand the woman's body, the more they learn to appreciate and reverence her fertility. This understanding helps a woman to control the feelings related to bodily changes rather than to be controlled by them.

An awareness of fertility is essential to the practice of Natural Family Planning, which is the loving method of birth control the Catholic Church teaches to be worthy of the dignity of persons.

Through this method, couples learn to live with their fertility as a positive reality in their lives. Their awareness of the signs of fertility enables them to plan their family responsibly in a morally acceptable and medically safe manner. With this knowledge, couples desiring a pregnancy can choose to have intercourse during the time of peak fertility when conception is most likely, or, if not desiring pregnancy, during the infertile time when conception will not occur.

Secular sex education, which focuses only upon the avoidance of pregnancy and veneral disease, fails to provide students with a positive view of the physiological dimensions of their sexuality. They are left with the impression that the menstrual cycle is a disease to be eradicated rather than a miracle of creation. Women and men must learn to appreciate the rhythms of the menstrual cycle and its influence upon certain biological functions. This appreciation comes from female fertility awareness, revolving around knowledge of when ovulation is about to occur, is occurring, and has occurred.

The miracle of the human body is again evident when it is realized that the unpregnant uterus can hold only a teaspoon of fluid. Yet, when the woman becomes pregnant, it expands to hold a quart of amniotic fluid which protects the child growing within. The woman's body miraculously adapts to provide "growing room" for this child whose heart can be heard to beat about three weeks after conception and from whom brain waves can be detected after six weeks. The child does not lie quietly within the womb but moves around, and the uterus adapts to all the exercise. Even though the quart of fluid is lost just prior to birth, the woman does not dehydrate.

This description of the scientific basis for Natural Family Planning has been deliberately incomplete, and no effort has been made to describe how to observe the various signs of fertility and infertility. All of this and more is spelled out in *The Art of Natural Family Planning.*[9]

---

[5]Myers, Kevin, "Kolbe' to Open at Dublin's Abbey," *Immaculata,* Aug. 1982. pp. 18-19.

[6]Rudolf Vollman, M.D. explains that it takes an average of sixty cycles for a woman's menstrual cycle to mature and about a score as she slows down in menopause. A woman will have about four hundred cycles during her lifetime.

[7]John T. Ball and Nancy Cashman Ball, *Joy in Sexuality: The Natural Way of Married Life,* Collegeville, Minn.: The Liturgical Press, 1975, pp. 52-54.

[8]Ball, p.54

[9]John and Sheila Kippley, The Art of Natural Family Planning, Couple to Couple League, Box 11084, Cincinnati, OH 45211.

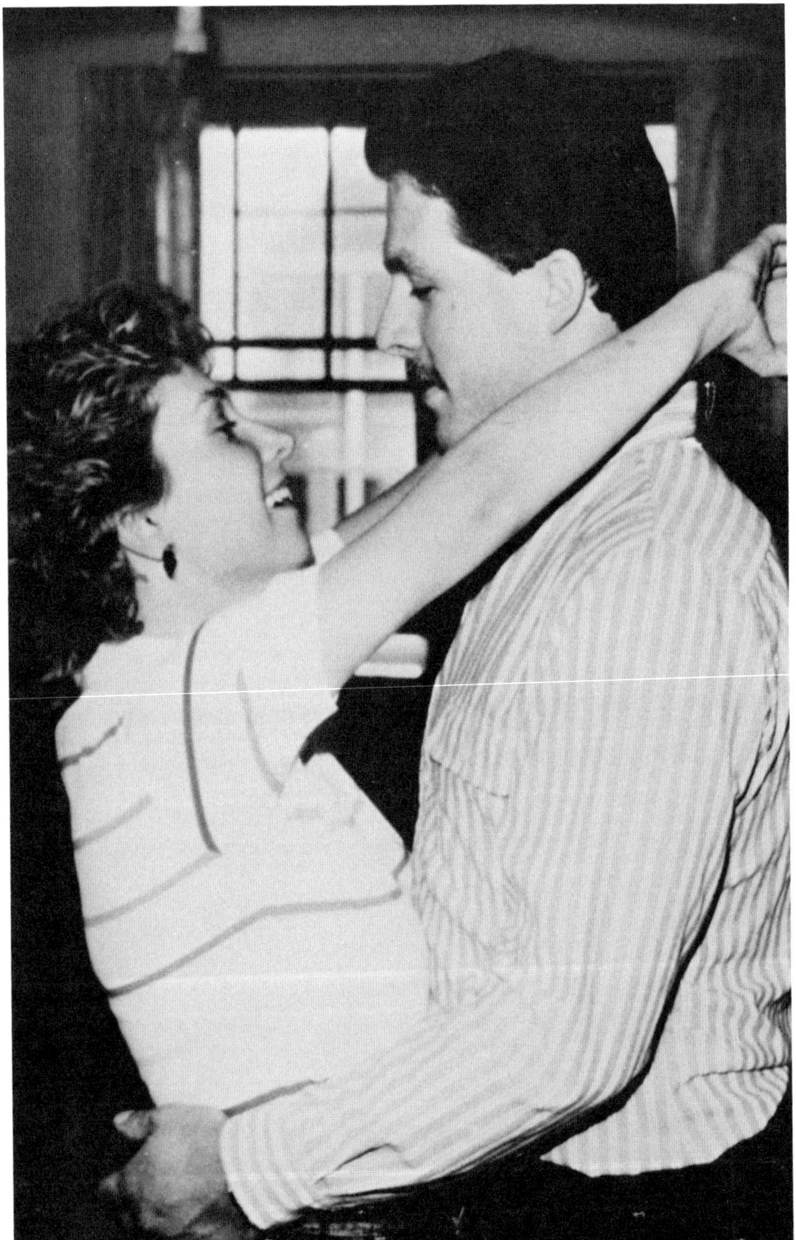

*CHAPTER 5*

# Resolving Differences

The friends of John and Mary, who have been married for fifteen years, would be surprised to find them sitting in the office of a marriage and family therapist where Mary tearfully asked her husband, "When did you stop loving me?" A very alarmed John asked, "What do you mean, stopped loving you?" Mary exlaimed, "You never tell me that you love me." Since deeds are more frequently important to men, John, a carpenter, was confused by her complaint and exclaimed, "I go out every day and work hard for a living. It is miserably cold and the work is so tough that my hands are all cut up. Doesn't that tell you that I love you?" Although he was amazed that his wife could not *see* that he loved her, she felt alone because he did not *say* he loved her.

It is not unusual for a husband and father to be standing near a ringing telephone. However, rather than to answer it himself, he may make a general announcement to the household, "The phone is ringing!" It is also quite possible that he will ask his wife to call the O'Briens to get together for bridge, and it is quite likely that his wife is responsible for most of the correspondence and especially for getting out the Christmas cards. One wife was unable to accompany her husband to Mass on a day that a visiting priest was celebrating the Mass and giving the homily. When the husband returned home, his wife asked, "Did you have the visiting priest?"

He: "Yes."

She: "Did he give the sermon?"

He: "Yes."

She: "What did he preach about?"

He: "Sin."

The wife asked what he said about sin and the husband replied, "He was against it."

Of course, one notices this lack of dependence upon words long prior to marriage. If you walk into an elementary classroom, it is quite possible one will find that the girls are more advanced in basic communication skills and that the boys will be poking and shoving one another around. During retreats with senior high school students, girls will frequently introduce themselves to me explaining that their parents have asked them to convey their greetings. Boys, who are considerably less verbal, seem to slouch in and move to the back of the room where they think there will be no danger of being called upon to talk in public. As engaged couples enter a conference room for the beginning of a weekend retreat, the women are often more verbal than the men who give a pretty clear message that others ought not to become too familiar with them until they are "checked out" and the seminar leaders can be trusted. Men, being more leery, seem to be saying, "Don't push it, fella. Give me some time to see if I am going to be able to take to you."

Although to an extent it may be true that women may rely more upon words and men upon actions, it would be unjustified to conclude, "That's the way it is and nothing can be done about it." Considering the spirit of complementarity, men may be called upon to see the value of putting their feelings into words and of letting their spouses know how they feel. When one couple appeared in domestic relations court, the judge asked the wife, "Why is it that after twenty-five years you are divorcing your husband?"

The wife replied, "Because he doesn't love me."

When the judge asked the husband whether or not it was true that he did not love his wife, the husband mumbled, "Of course not! I told her twenty-five years ago I loved her and I haven't taken it back since." It may be important for the wife to hear the expression of love a little more often than every twenty-five years. In the same vein, it may be important for women to recognize that, in many instances, actions speak louder than words. Many husbands, who are deeply devoted to their wives, show that devotion by living out a life of day-to-day commitment. Unfortunately, some wives may fail to hear the "I love you" inherent in the actions.

In a vein that may be more concerned with the niceties and details of life, seventeen year-old Peter gave his girlfriend an unwrapped gift and was hurt because she was not as excited as he thought she would be. When he mentioned this to his mother, she helped him understand that wrapping the gift and having a card to go along with it would have meant much more to Tanya. When Peter exclaimed, "Now I know what Dad is talking about when he says, 'You can never understand a woman.' " He was beginning to understand sexual differences.

On the other hand, Tanya's father will need to explain to her that she must understand how important it was for Peter to be able to give her the gift and that she needs to appreciate the meaning behind the giving of the gift. Although the way something is done is very important to a woman, the man may simply want to get the job done. Since little things may mean more to a woman, she may fuss with the table setting and the man may be satisfied to get the food on the table and eat. This can present some tension as a couple prepares to entertain guests or as they are preparing for the holidays. While the wife may be very concerned about everything looking special, the husband may be concerned that she is neglecting their relationship.

Learning to appreciate and understand sexual differences is a part of the challenge during engagement and remains a challenge throughout all the years of marriage. Love is expressed through a continuing recognition of the need to understand one's own sexuality, that of the other sex, and the way in which the sexes complement each other. According to the creation story in Genesis, God said it is not good for man to be alone and He created a woman to be Adam's helpmate. Saying that a woman's tenderness complements a man's physical strength does not imply that the unmarried are incomplete but only that both sexes play a different role in building God's Kingdom.

Whether or not a woman marries or ever becomes pregnant, it remains true that her body and psyche are geared to the conception, birth, and rearing of children. The ears of an infant are better attuned to the mother's soprano voice than to the bass voice of the father. A mother and infant babble away and seemingly understand each other.

The advent of the Yuppie (young urban professionals) culture and their gross materialism can cause one to question the "across the board" desire of women to have a home and family. The contrast between couples was evident during a discussion with engaged couples when one couple explained, "We have a dual-career problem. I want to live in Minneapolis where my job is, and she wants to remain in Chicago where her job is." Another couple said, "We also have a dual-career problem. I want to be Mr. Mom and she wants to be Mrs. Mom."

It does seem that many married women have a deeply embedded desire to bear a child by the man they love. In an age atrociously affected by an anti-life philosophy, it is sad to hear a husband reject his wife's gentle request for a baby. When she begins to beg for a baby, some husbands play God as they refuse to "let her have a baby." On the other hand, there are women who, having been duped by the anti-life component of the feminist movement, deny their innate desire for a baby and who refuse the husband who pleads to let them have a baby. Modern women and men who are cursing their fertility are rebelling against a desire God has placed deep within them.

Since a woman is less muscular than a man, is physically less strong and less suited for strenuous physical labor, it is a perversion of equality to say that men and women should perform the same jobs. Equality involves acceptance of a person for his or her talents and not the application of some universalized standard declaring that everyone has to be alike. One wife angrily complained that she would not sew buttons on her husband's shirts, saying he was not crippled and was as capable as her of putting on buttons. This misses the point of complementarity. Since a woman's fingers are generally smaller and better able to cope with minute and delicate tasks, she may be better suited to sewing than is her husband.

## Masculine and Feminine Complements

There are some indications that men and women have a different approach to their spiritual life. It appears that a woman's greater receptivity, coupled with a greater capacity for passivity, may free her for a deeper spiritual life. The tendency of males to compartmentalize, coupled with an attitude of strict self-reliance, creates resistances that need to be overcome. A woman may simultaneously be able to serve the soup, listen to the homework assignment, and contemplate God's activity in her life. Women also seem to be more reflective and able to be caught up in God's love while men are trying to figure Him out.

Again, the differences are complementary as God has given men and women different but necessary talents, enabling them to develop rewarding spiritual lives. In their roles as helpmates, men and women have the inherent potential to help each other discover a closer union with God. Although one cannot overlook the theological contributions of women such as Catherine of Siena and Teresa of Avila, there have been many more male than female theologians and many more female than male contemplatives. However, it must also be recognized that, in earlier times, women were denied the opportunity to study as theologians. Yet, we do see male-female combinations in which each person contributed significantly to the spiritual development of the other. To this day, many of us profit from the complementary nature of their differences.

Students of Benedictine education and others may recall the loving relationship between St. Benedict and his sister St. Scholastica, saints who worked and prayed in the Fifth and Sixth Centuries. At the time of her last visit with her brother, St. Scholastica pleaded with Benedict to stay and talk with her a little longer. He protested that he had to hasten back to work at the monastery. With that, St. Scholastica looked towards the heavens and after a few moments of prayer, they broke loose with thunder and lightening. Recognizing that there was no way he was going to make it back to the monastery, Benedict turned to his sister exclaiming, "I should know better than to ever get between you and God."

The founders of the Franciscan Order and of the Poor Clares, St. Francis and St. Clare, had a relationship which 800 years later continues to pay dividends to us. Others may especially remember the relationship between the rather shy St. John of the Cross and the articulate and charismatic Teresa of Avila. Teresa, who was larger in stature, referred to St. John, who was one of the spiritual advisors, as her half-priest. The different approaches these saints had to serving God and their understanding of him, emphasize different truths of God. Each emphasis helps us to develop a more total understanding of God.

As people mature emotionally and spiritually, it is quite likely that men will assume many of the characteristics often identified with femininity. However, rather than appearing effeminate, they will, in the process of assuming these traits, appear all the more masculine. They will become real *gentle* men. As a woman matures emotionally and spiritually, it is quite likely that she will integrate many of the traits frequently associated with masculinity. However, rather than appear "butchy," she appears all the more feminine—more of a *gentle* woman.

This conclusion is quite reasonable. As we grow in virtue—as we grow spiritually and emotionally—it is reasonable to expect that we will come to resemble more closely the image of the God in whom we have been created. Since God encompasses and reflects all of what is considered to be masculine and feminine, we can assume that, as we more closely reflect his image, we will also reflect characteristics attributable to each of the sexes. Thus, as engaged couples and as spouses help each other appreciate their own sexuality as well as the sexuality of the other, they are helping each other to become more human—to become more saintly—to become more of what they were created to be—reflections of the image and likeness of God.

about how the other's sense of humor is embarrassing to them. e persons laugh from the tips of their toes to the top of their . In fact, their laugh may come out as more of a gasp, and it may be all that unusual for them to double over in laughter. Others smile or emit a little "huh." Sometimes you can measure how y something may be by whether or not persons, not usually n to outbusts of laughter, will actually laugh out loud. Engaged les who are embarrassed by their partner's laughter or sense of or, may kick their partner in the shins so frequently that the her may have to either get a pair of shin pads or move to another of the room.

Not only are couples different in their sense of humor, but also in way they have learned to express emotions. Alice celebrated her nty-third birthday after we had been married for seven months. en she came home she found that I had prepared a lovely hot , a sheet birthday cake that was nicely decorated and a generic hday card. After a couple of bites of hot dish (our favorite book the first few years of marriage was *365 Different Ways to Use nburger* ) she began to cry. Since I was a first year student in the duate School of Social Work, I opened a text book to page fifty ere I found advice for helping someone who was crying. When I ed Alice what was wrong, she replied, "Nothing." Being guided my textbook, I exclaimed, "You usually don't sit around the se crying. The hot dish isn't that bad. There must be something ong." She said, "Well, *it is my birthday*." I explained that the hot h, cake and card were dead giveaways that I was aware of that.

Although my own family was more emotive than Alice's, we er made a special celebration out of birthdays or anniversaries. wever, Alice's family made a special celebration out of these casions. She expected that I would have invited her sister and her nily to join us for a birthday dinner or that we would have gone t to dinner. Although it is generally true that we adapt and adjust to ferences, there are times when one party changes simply because y prefer the other's way. It did not take very many birthdays fore I changed to Alice's way. Over the years, I have greatly joyed the wonderful birthday parties and anniversary celebrations have had.

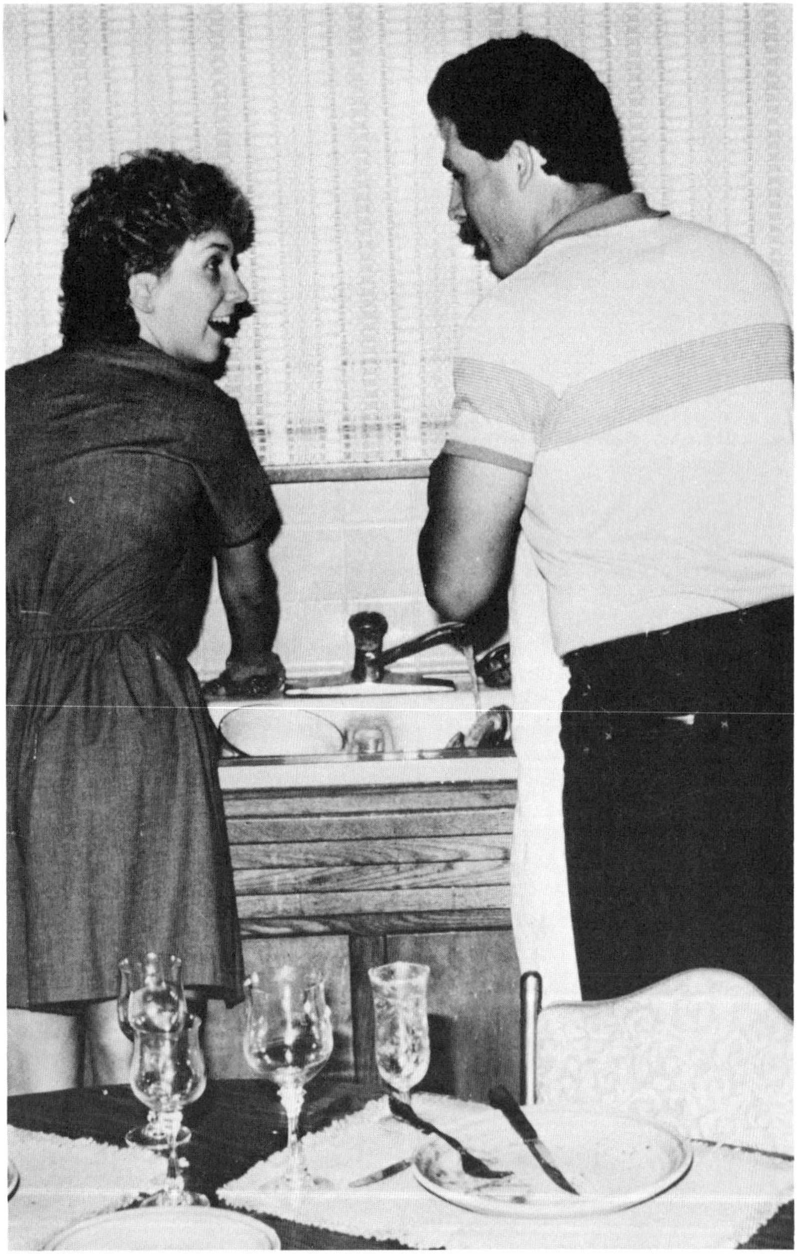

*CHAPTER 6*

# Making Adjustme

As partners are challenged to understand the nature of their sexuality, they are challenged to different ideas about living can also become an develop oneness.

When two people anticipate marriage, they are sc man who had been born and raised in France and t had been born and raised in Germany. Each of the years learning their own language of behavior. Now marrying, they needed to develop a language comi them. Most couples have spent several years learning and how to laugh, what to celebrate and how to cele to mourn and how to mourn. The problem is that each idea of what is funny and a different idea of how to la idea of what to celebrate, a different way in which to different idea of what to mourn and how to express s

Partners need to talk about how they fail to a other's sense of humor. Although it may be sensitiv

The occasion of her twenty-third birthday was simply the beginning of our coming to appreciate the difference between our Frenchness and Germanness. A few years later we were just about within sight of the silo on her parent's farm when our three-year-old daughter commented, "Let me see, we are going to visit Grandpa and Grandma Lehar. They will shake my hand. It is Grandpa and Grandma Quesnell who kiss me." Alice and I looked at each other realizing that our daughter had just explained the reason for a good deal of our tension.

Alice and I had gone together for several months before her parents would even shake my hand. On the other hand, when my Irish mother met Alice, she immediately threw her arms around her and hugged and kissed her. Poor Alice, being unaccustomed to such forwardness, broke out in the hives.

This illustration of the difference in our use of language has had tremendous implications for our marriage. After living in our 27 x 8 foot mobile home for a couple of years and then graduating to a 50 x 10 for the next five years, we finally had saved enough money to go into debt. So after seven years of marriage, we began looking for a house. Having been considerably humbled by previous mistakes, we asked Alice's parents to look at the home. As we stood in the driveway, my father-in-law said, "Jack, we are really very pleased with how hard you and Alice have been working and we want to help you out by giving you $5,000 as a down payment." Remember that this occurred in 1965 when $5,000 constituted one-sixth of the price of our home.

However, my own family background was such that, when someone offered to do something unusual for me, I generally offered a cursory refusal but did not intend the person to take me seriously. Thus, I said, "No, Grandpa, that's okay. We can make it." I was terribly chagrined to find that my father-in-law did not know his lines. I expected him to say, "Aw, come on, don't be so proud, we want to help you out, please take it." Unfortunately he became embarrassed thinking that he had insulted me, and he was hurt that I had refused his generous offer. However, once offered, and unintentionally refused, the subject was closed.

Couples may find out that their families also have different ideas about the way in which Christmas should be celebrated. Faced with these differences, they may feel that to celebrate Christmas in any different way would be tantamount to an act of treason against their family. Some families believe packages are opened on Christmas Eve, and others think that Christmas Eve is spent getting ready for Christmas Day. Then a large meal is served, and packages are opened sometime in the early afternoon.

Couples need only to consider some of the tension revolving around their wedding plans to gain an appreciation of the different ways in which families celebrate. Some families believe a wedding is not properly celebrated unless everyone down to the fifth cousin is invited. Others place more emphasis upon a small intimate wedding. Some couples and families may disagree about whether or not children are to be invited. One man who came from a large family was the last one in his family to marry. Thus, he had a number of nephews and nieces. The woman, having no nephews and nieces, thought children would spoil the beautiful liturgy, elegant reception and dinner. The man's family was offended by the thought that children would not be a part of the celebration.

For some families, the dancing, eating and drinking begins as soon as the couple walks out of the church and continues well into the next day. In some families, the actual wedding, reception, dinner and dance is one day of celebration, and the opening of gifts is the next day's celebration. Some families include all the young children on the guest list and others intend an adults-only wedding. Some families believe a wedding is not valid unless alcohol flows freely, and other families may think it nearly sacrilegious to serve alcohol at a wedding.

I have the opportunity to be involved in marriage preparation in an area of the country where there is an ethnic group of German-Russians and another group of Norwegians. The German-Russians who are Catholics seem to think that they are obligated to drink in order to prove they are not Baptist and to validate the marriage. In fact, they have a traditional wedding drink that is made with 190 proof alcohol. When a German-Russian marries a Norwegian who is Lutheran, he or she may come from a family which, operates on the principle, "My lips have never touched alcohol and never will touch those that have touched alcohol." Not only would the Norwegian family be scandalized by the drinking, but they may think they will pass out if they so much as inhale the wedding drink.

One woman complained that since her fiancé's "old man was too cheap to buy the booze, my father is going to buy it all. If there is no booze, there will be no wedding!" As the man sat somewhat sheepishly, he explained that alcohol had been a serious problem for some members of his family and that, out of respect for those who were trying to abstain from alcohol, his family preferred not to make alcohol available. Another woman, who was much less brazen, and whose fiancé was a member of Alcoholics Anonymous, simply explained that her family would feel great embarrassment if alcohol were not present. They were concerned that their friends would think they were cheap.

It is important to appreciate that for some families, alcohol is simply associated with joy. However, for other families, alcohol has been experienced as terrible suffering. If one of the families has serious reservations about the availability of alcohol at the celebration, that reservation should be seriously considered. The sensitivity shown in the way the wedding is to be celebrated may be an indication of the sensitivity that will be shown in the situations that will arise during the first sixty years of marriage. Since different ideas about how the wedding will be celebrated are only a small indication of the differences that will be encountered in marriage, it is important to deal directly with them. They provide opportunities to rehearse the way they will be dealt with during the next sixty years. Because of an effort to establish their own identity, a couple that is about to marry may agree that some of the expectations of their families are kind of kooky. However, they will not be far into their marriage before they find themselves fervently and jealously defending the customs of their individual families. Then, the other spouse dare not attack these "sacred traditions."

This may also be the time to mention that it is all right for a spouse to complain about his or her own family. But, it is very risky to criticize the family of one's spouse. It is even risky to respond to complaints one's spouse has about his or her own family. If you agree too enthusiastically, you may be asked, "And what business do you have berating my family?" If you do not agree, you may be accused of "Never sticking up for me."

It is also wise to be cautious about how much you tell your family about your own domestic squabbles. If you tell your family too many intimate details and too much about the hurt you may have experienced, it may be more difficult for them to forgive. The relationship spouses have with each other is very different than the one in-laws have with them. Spouses may squabble, pout for a while, apologize and kiss and make up. It may not be that easy for in-laws to be reconciled with a son-in-law or daughter-in-law.

The main point of these comments regarding in-laws is that differences about the size of the wedding may be an indication of the size of family reunions and the extent to which attendance will be "mandatory." One husband who came from a relatively small family had a difficult time adjusting to the visits to the family of his wife. She came from a large family which placed heavy emphasis upon togetherness. Whenever he and his wife and children went to visit her parents, the parents invited all the other children and grandchildren (twenty-five of them) to also come and stay. When the husband suggested that he and his family stay in a motel, the family of the wife was offended and felt that he thought he was too good to sleep on the floor and to stand in line to go to the bathroom. For the interfaith couple, concern about the church in which the wedding will be celebrated is a beginning for dealing with the baptism and confirmation of the children.

The indiscretion of overextending the piece of folklore that opposites attract was demonstrated by the woman who exclaimed, "Oh, my fiancé and I are so different that we are just made for each other. He is shy, and has low energy, and is close with money. I am a dancer in a night club, I am outgoing, and I love to spend money. While I see to it that we go out and have a chance to meet and be with others, Francis calms my restless spirit and sees to it that a little money is saved." Unfortunately, she overlooked the fact that significant differences influenced by sexuality offer a sufficient challenge to couples without superimposing radical differences in background, personality, values and life styles. Ignoring pleas to do each other the favor of not marrying, their marriage came to a tragic end.

On the occasion of my father's death, Alice and I realized that we had learned to react to death in very different ways. After the funeral, we were joined at the home of my mother by several close friends and relatives. One of my humorous uncles told one story after the other. I was literally doubled over with laughter. As the guests began to leave, I found Alice lying in bed crying. As I touched her and asked what was wrong, she very bitterly asked, "How can you ask what is wrong with me? What is wrong with you and Lowell? Don't the two of you even care for your dad? Here it is the day of your dad's funeral and the two of you are carrying on like a couple of fools!"

Then, I realized that Alice did not think people could be sad and happy at the same time. In reality, I had never really known what emotional pain was until my father died. The pain not only resulted from a sense of loss, but from a feeling of regret that I had never told him how much I cared for him and that I had never thanked him for all he had done. In my family, funerals had been rather joy-filled occasions where we saw old friends and relatives and caught up on the news and the most recent stories. In fact, some members of my family affectionately refer to funerals as "planting parties" and trips to the "marble orchard." However, I needed to realize that Alice's family reacted more somberly at funerals. On another occasion, I was out of order with one of the stories I told after the burial of one of her uncles who had served in World War I and for whom there had been a military honor guard. During the funeral brunch, I was met with a rather cold stare when I told of the funeral at a national cemetery where, when the first round was fired, the widow fainted away on the spot. As she fell to the ground, a sixth grader gasped, "Jesus Christ! They shot Grandma!"

A few days after my father's funeral, Alice's folks came to our home for Thanksgiving. I was insulted that they did not ask about his death or about my mother. They carried on as usual. Even when they talked with my mother on the telephone, they did not ask anything about the death. When Alice and I went to bed, I asked, "What in the devil is happening to your parents? The older they get the more selfish they become. Unless you are talking about their bowels and their bladder, they could care less." Alice replied that she did not know what was happening. A couple of days later, as we were returning from having taken them to their home, Alice said, "After twenty-two years of marriage, we are still learning about our differences. Whenever you were gone, my folks showed great concern about you, your mother, and the rest of the family." We had to understand that their silence to me was actually a sign of respect and concern. In their way of dealing with emotions, a man's grief was his own. They respected my privacy and did not pry.

In so many instances, what is intended as a show of concern by one spouse is interpreted as a lack of concern by the other. If spouses fail to understand each other's language, they will be condemned to a life of hurt, resentment, and misunderstanding. For instance, a boy grew up being too embarrassed to invite friends into his home. Although he had a bed in which to sleep, he shared it with a couple of brothers and they shared the room with sisters. Although they had food to eat, it was a rather sparse diet. Not having clothes with the right designer labels, he was the brunt of jokes by his classmates. Thankfully, a teacher took a special interest in him and helped him understand that education was the way out of his predicament. As a young boy, he decided that, no matter what the effort, he was going to graduate from college. After that he intended to find a good job with a large company in which advancement was possible.

Somewhere along the way he met a woman who had different experiences. Although she did not have a room of her own, she did have her own bed and while her family ate a lot of hot dish, she was not embarrassed to share her home with her friends. Her clothes were generally the "right kind," her father was home almost every evening, and he went to all the parent-teacher conferences, to the games, plays and concerts.

They became engaged. He found a good job and they began their married life. He learned that if he was going to give his family extras, and if he was going to climb to the top in his company, it would be necessary to work sixty or seventy hours a week. Each child had his or her own bedroom. They had plenty of steak and they took a week or two of vacation in the summer and again in the winter. However, other than the rather exotic vacations, the father was pretty much absent from the scene. Thinking he was married to his job, his wife began to retreat and isolate herself in her own cocoon. When the husband misunderstood her message, he began to work more thinking that if he could climb further, gain more status, and bring home more money, then she would act lovingly towards him. Fortunately, they were able to recognize that something was going wrong and they sought the help of a marriage counselor who helped them understand each other's language. The wife could only joyfully cry, "You mean you were really doing all those things because you *loved* me and the children?"

During engagement, couples who fail to see the differences between them, do not recognize that, in some ways, they are speaking a different language. Some of this failure to see differences may be because they may not be seeing much of each other. There are other couples who may recognize their differences, but push them aside saying, "It really does not make any difference," or "If I really love him/her, I won't care about things like that." This explanation evolves from the myth that love makes all differences inconsequential. However, underneath it all, many engaged persons mean something like, "Although he/she does some funny things, I am certain that after we are married and spend more time together, I will be able to teach him or her the proper way to live."

This reaction is based upon a belief that "I am a mature person who is intelligent enough to make a good decision about marriage. Now although my partner is also mature and intelligent, there are some things about life that he/she has not had the opportunity to learn. However, since he/she is smart, I know he/she will be open to learning a better and more effective way in which to live." Unfortunately, this self-satisfied person is unaware that the partner is thinking the same thing.

This sense of self-satisfaction comes from having lived life rather successfully and from not being burdened by any major regrets. "As long as my way has worked, it must be a good way and if it is good for me, it ought to be good for my partner." This attitude is based upon the principle of any auto mechanic who firmly believes, "If it works, don't fix it." However, such self-satisfaction overlooks the fact that the other person is also satisfied with the way in which his/her life has gone. This can be a special problem for engaged couples who are well into their twenties. Couples in this age group may not only feel that they have done very well with their life, but they may have enough successful years behind them to have become set in their ways.

## The Language of Behavior

A second characteristic of our unique language is that we are unaware of the language we speak. For instance, we seldom say, "Isn't it convenient that the person speaks English." For those of us who are accustomed to speaking English, it does not occur to us that others are doing us the favor of speaking a language we understand. We simply expect to be understood and we would take our business elsewhere if we did not speak the same language. Thus, it does not occur to an engaged individual that his/her partner is not understanding his/her behavior. This language of behavior is deeply embedded within us and is expressed as a conditioned reflex. We react to stimuli as we have been "trained" to react.

A related characteristic is that, in times of crisis, we tend to call upon an earlier language. For instance, a nurse explained that the head nurse on their floor had been born and raised in South America. Although she spoke fluent English, whenever there was a crisis on the floor, she would begin speaking Spanish. Her colleagues would say, "We can't understand you. Please speak English." With absolute astonishment, she would say, "I am speaking English."

If couples have grown up with parents or grandparents who were born and raised in a foreign country, they might find that profane words are the only words they have learned from their parents' or grandparents' native tongue. That is because whenever the parents or grandparents were confronted with a frustrating situation, they called for "God's assistance" in their native tongue. In the late 1970's, a man named Gary Gilmore was condemned to die by a firing squad of the Utah State Prison. Somewhere in his background he had been a Catholic and he had, in fact, served Mass in the days when Mass was offered in Latin. Although he had been away from the church for many years, he did return some time prior to his execution. When Mass was celebrated in his cell on the day before his execution, the Chaplain and the prison guard commented that is was a very moving celebration of the Eucharist. On the day of his execution, he stood before the firing squad. As he was about to be offered a blindfold, the chaplain asked him, "Mr. Gilmore, do you have any last words?" In this time of crisis, and years after he had heard any Latin, he reached back to a time when life was more pleasant for him and replied, "Dominus vobiscum." The priest immediately responded, "Et cum Spiritu tuo." His earlier language was appropriate, for when greeted with "The Lord be with you," the response is, "And with your Spirit also."

The fact that a crisis frequently causes us to call upon an earlier language has special relevance for the engaged. Although this statement is not intended to have negative implications for marriage, it is simply a fact that marriage is a crisis. Newlyweds may find themselves calling upon reactions and behaviors that they thought had long been forgotten. They may also find themselves thinking it strange that spouses do things they had not previously seen them do or heard them say. Once, as I was turning into a gate at the airport, a couple who had just returned from their honeymoon in Hawaii came running up to greet me. As we visited about the Engaged Conference they had attended several months earlier, the bride politely excused herself to go to the restroom. When she was out of earshot, the man said, "Am I ever grateful for that session we had about differences. I never imagined she would do so many dumb things."What she was doing was not dumb—just different. Also, during this time of critical transition, she was calling upon responses that were totally foreign to her husband. Marriage is a time of critical transition in which couples are required to make many adaptations and adjustments.

*CHAPTER 7*

# Adapting to Differences

Although the differences in language lead to misunderstandings about major issues such as death, how love is expressed, and how a wedding ought to be celebrated, couples will find that a good bit of marital tension is caused by absolute trivia. Although this book does not describe complex psychological problems, recall that problems represent those situations and/or behaviors requiring change. Although most happily married and mature couples find that trivia is enough to drive them up a tree, they are generally able to find a way to deal with it. The fact that trivia can be so pesky indicates how essential it is to resolve problems and to identify irreconciliable differences before marriage. They can be absolutely devastating to a marriage.

On one level, it is important that couples resolve basic value issues. For instance, it can be very disconcerting to a marriage if one spouse places more emphasis upon job or career than upon marriage and if the other gives more priority to marriage and family life. The partner to whom religion and religious practices are very important will be very lonely and unhappy if he/she marries someone who is indifferent or hostile to religion. It is hard to understand the lack of discretion of a strong Christian who intends to marry an agnostic, atheist, or a luke-warm Christian. Of course, luke-warm Christians frequently can be more difficult in marriage than an atheist or agnostic.

It is important to have a common commitment to children to care for and to educate. One middle-age couple could not understand why they never had any money. When they began to count how much money they were spending for their children to attend parochial schools and private colleges, they understood why their money was not stretching. Had they not shared a common value about education, one could have blamed the other for the cash shortage, saying, "If it wasn't for your dumb ideas about education, we would have enough money to do some really important things like taking a Caribbean cruise." If they had attended different schools and had academic, social or behavior problems, the other spouse could have said, "If they had attended different schools, our children would have been spared these problems."

One can imagine the tension between spouses if one partner wants to use Natural Family Planning and the other partner insists upon contraceptive birth control. Strong emphasis has been placed upon the need to adapt and adjust to situations in which neither is wrong and yet the parties are diametrically opposed. Sometimes differences are so extreme that they will interfere with the kind of satisfaction and companionship couples can reasonably expect in marriage. One person may be very active, outgoing, and involved in various activities while the other may strongly prefer that they spend more time sitting around by themselves rather than "always to have to be with other people and be on the run." One may believe in the discrete use of credit and the other may be irrevocably opposed to charging anything. It must be recognized that some personality and lifestyle differences are so extreme that adaptation is not feasible. I cannot emphasize too strongly that it is essential to resolve problems revolving around alcohol and drug abuse, immaturity, mental illness, selfishness, and verbal or physical abuse. Any doubt about the need to resolve problems in these areas satisfactorily will be put to rest if one has the opportunity to talk to the tragic victims of the spouses burdened by any of these problems.

A nagging concern about irreconcilable differences and problems can contribute to the phenomenon frequently referred to as pre-nuptial jitters. These jitters should not be dismissed with simplistic comments such as "you will get over it," "everyone feels that way," or "I felt that way too and am happy I did not change my mind." In assessing the meaning of the jitters, the couples experiencing them should assess the extent to which they normally become upset over major events such as examinations, graduation, job interviews, or new jobs. If he or she usually becomes upset, but proceeds through the experience and is happy for having done so, the pre-nuptial jitters may not warrant cancelling the wedding.

But if jitters are quite out of proportion to what the individual usually experiences, it will be necessary to examine thoroughly all the dynamics that could be contributing to the development of the feelings. These dynamics could involve the nature of the engaged relationship and/or the personality makeup of one or both of the partners. It may be that one or both of them have had chronic doubts about the relationship, but just went along with the engagement because it seemed to be too much of a hassle to breakup. Now that the marriage "is just around the corner," they realize it is time to make a decision. Painful as it may be to call off a wedding, it will be infinitely more painful to enter into an ill-advised marriage. Because the invitations have been mailed, shower gifts have been received and the downpayment has been made for the reception hall, an unwise marriage is not justified. Nothing should force anyone to marry. People must be as free not to marry as they are to marry.

If thorough analysis of the feelings reveal an absence of serious problems in the relationship and an absence of chronic and nagging doubts, it may be that the jitters are only indicative of an expected nervousness about a major event.

There is a tendency to think that, since we are mature and intelligent, we should not become upset about issues as trivial as how toothpaste is squeezed, how a peanut butter and jelly sandwich is made, and whether or not a toilet seat is put down. However, if a couple is going to learn to understand each other, they must be humble enough to admit that they can become upset about absolute trivia. Unfortunately, we tend to treat trivia like a grain of sand in our shoe. When a grain of sand gets into our shoe, we may think, "How can such a little pebble hurt? I am bigger than that, I won't let it bother me, it really doesn't hurt." Instead of being sensible, taking off our shoe and shaking out the grain of sand, many of us hobble and limp around trying to kick our foot in such a way that the sand won't irritate.

One couple, who was in their mid to late twenties, became insulted when, during a retreat for the engaged, it was suggested that it could be terribly frustrating to be married to someone lacking in an aesthetic appreciation for a tube of toothpaste. If one partner did not appreciate that toothpaste was to be squeezed from the bottom of the tube and that the used portion was to be rolled up a couple of times a week, then neither would he/she care where the toothpaste landed. For instance, it might land in the sink where it would get mixed up with gobs of hair, or it may land on the floor where it might get caught up between one's toes. As they left that session, the woman commented, "That guy is really a simpleton. He cannot believe that mature people like us are going to argue about something as dumb as a tube of toothpaste." Although there is an advantage in being older, one of the risks is that each of the partners will have become set in their ways. They each may be strongly committed to the idea that there are two ways to do things—my way and the wrong way. This couple later said, "Two years of marriage has taught us that the toothpaste is only one of 200 irritating pieces of trivia frustrating our lives. There were an infinite number of other items such as:

1. At what temperature should the thermostat be set?
2. Should the bedroom windows be open?
3. Should we have an electric blanket or a down comforter?
4. How do you prepare a meal?
5. What do you prepare for a meal?
6. How do you wash dishes?
7. Should butter and margarine be kept in the refrigerator or out on the countertop?

During the course of a marriage retreat, one couple asked if I could guess the most pressing problem they had experienced during their first five years of marriage. After a few futile guesses, I found that the direction in which the toilet tissue should roll was the most confounding issue they faced. After hearing this, I announced to another group that I had a tremendous French-German type example for them. When I explained how I could not imagine how it could make any difference whether the tissue hung from the back or the front, a woman rose to disagree exclaiming, "It does make a difference. You obviously have forgotten what it is like to have toddlers. If the tissue is hanging from the back, they can turn the roll all day long and it just goes around and around. However, if it is hanging from the front, they can T.P. your house in five minutes."

Having been told that there was a rational and logical explanation for doing it one way rather than another, I announced to another group that there was an answer to the toilet tissue issue. When the answer was explained, another woman objected exclaiming, "It should hang from the front!" When I meekly asked, "Why?" she explained that, "Then people do not get fingermarks on the wall."

The fact that love is demonstrated by a willingness to be concerned about little things is quickly appreciated by the woman married to a man who came from a family of brothers. She found that her most disconcerting problem revolved around leaving the toilet seat in the up position. This did not assume paramount concern until she was about eight months pregnant. Awakened about 2:00 a.m. with the little one doing a polka on her bladder, she stumbled to the bathroom only to find that life is, indeed, a game of inches and that an inch and a half makes all the difference in the world.

How many men who would be willing to swim the deepest ocean, cross the driest desert and climb the highest mountain to prove their love, ever thought that the ultimate proof of love would revolve around remembering to put down the toilet seat? It is unfair to surface such pressing issues without offering feasible solutions. We have found couples open to the suggestion that the person who hangs the toilet tissue chooses the side from which it will be hung. The toilet seat issue can be solved by using a fabric-type toilet seat cover that is sufficiently thick to prevent the cover from resting against the water tank.

However, conscientious men may quickly object that they will be unable to accurately direct the "flow" with one hand if they have to hold the cover with the other. Thank heaven for small favors because this leads to the solution of a related problem. No matter how accurate the man is, he will, inevitably, experience a splash problem. But, if the depth of his love brings him to genuflect or kneel at the "porcelain altar," he will, without splash, be able to hold up the leaning cover while directing the flow.

During the initial years of our marriage, Alice and I enjoyed doing dishes together. During my early years as a marriage counselor, there was a tendency to believe that if something worked for me, it should work for everyone. While operating under that delusion, I tended to suggest that marriages could be enriched if spouses would do dishes together. I was surprised to learn the number of different ways in which people thought dishes should be done and the depth of investment they had in doing dishes their way. There are those who change dish water two or three times during the washing and some who think dishes should be dried with a towel while others think they should be allowed to drip dry. Some rather naive people think an automatic dishwasher will solve the problem. However, this only provides spouses with the opportunity to argue about how clean the dishes should be before they are put into the dishwasher, how the dishes should go in the dishwasher, whether or not the dishwasher should be completely filled before being turned on and at which point the dishes should be removed from the dishwasher.

Of course, there are numerous arguments revolving around the number of utensils that should be used in preparing a meal and when the kitchen should be cleaned. Those hassles are nothing compared to those revolving around what should be eaten for a meal. For instance, when a couple returns from their honeymoon, the wife may decide to stay home from work a few extra days in order to turn their little house or apartment into a warm and loving home. Soon after her husband goes off for a hard day of physical labor, she may go shopping to buy some fresh vegetables and beef. She may be able to purchase a fresh avocado for the fresh avocado dressing she will prepare in one of the five blenders they received as wedding gifts. She may buy other fresh vegetables for the salad and some fresh beef for the vegetable-beef soup she will prepare in one of the five crock pots they received as wedding gifts.

Then she may put on the linen tablecloth they received as a wedding gift along with the monogrammed linen napkins, the champagne bucket, and the champagne glasses with their initials. With the candelabra lighted and soft music playing, she waits expectantly for her husband. When he comes in, he heads for the bathroom to wash up. As he sits at the table, he may appear to inhale his champagne. His wife may become terribly disillusioned thinking that they would sip their champagne for at least a couple of hours.

Valiantly trying to recover from the shock, the wife may bring the salad to the table only to find that, too, is immediately woofed down. Still hoping for a romantic candlelight dinner, she brings the vegetable-beef soup only to find that inhaled, like the champagne. With that, the groom exclaims, "What's for supper?" His poor wife is devastated thinking that he didn't like her meal and that, therefore, he doesn't love her. On the other hand, the husband thinks his wife wants to starve him to death during the first year so she can collect on his life insurance policy. He is expecting a platter of meat, a bowl of potatoes, a bowl of gravy, two kinds of vegetables, dark and white bread, coffee and milk, pie and cake. The fact that he is not appreciating her meal has absolutely nothing to do with whether or not he loves her. He just wants to eat.

The same kind of misunderstanding can occur between spouses coming from large and small families. For instance, after an evening meal, a husband, who was an only child, may get up from the table explaining to his wife that he is going to go out for a walk and that he will be back in about fifteen minutes. He returns to find his wife sobbing. When he asks, "What is wrong?" she explains, "Nothing!" Whenever we say nothing, we can always be very certain that that nothing is a hard cold lump of something. He finally discovers that his wife is upset because he did not ask her to go along. When he explains, "I didn't ask you because I wanted to be alone," his wife is convinced he does not love her.

The fact that he wanted to be alone has nothing to do with whether he loves his wife. It may simply be that, coming from a smaller family, he is accustomed to more private time. His wife, coming from a larger family, would think that a plague had struck the home if people were not around and if there was not some kind of noise and distraction. She may have been eighteen years old before she found out that beds were made to be slept in lengthwise and not crosswise. She also may get up every morning at 5:00 in order to get first crack at the clothes. Most certainly, she gets to the table immediately to be sure there will be some food for her. She may have no qualms about keeping the bedroom light on to read or having the TV blaring, or talking on the phone, as he is trying to get to sleep.

The essential challenge revolves around making the differences work for, rather than against us. We found that our differences worked amazingly well for us on the evening we discovered water coming through the ceiling. We were watching the news before going to bed and planning to get up early the next morning to leave on a trip. Much of the news was about the unfortunate people whose basements were being flooded as a result of a couple of days of heavy rain. Alice and I watched rather self-righteously because we had been wise enough to solve the problem of water in our basement by installing drain tile and a sump pump. As the sump pump wooshed out the water, we smiled knowingly at each other and congratulated ourselves for being so visionary. Unfortunately, we should have realized that whenever we become self-satisfied, we are about two minutes away from disaster.

As we went upstairs and started across the living room floor, we heard, "Squish, squash, squish." We looked up, and saw water coming in through the ceiling. I immediately rushed out to the garage to get the stepladder. As I was twisting through the closet and pulling myself up into the attic, Alice came with her interminable questions, "What are you going to do?"

With great irritation, I asked, "What does it look like I am going to do? I am going to see where the water is coming in!" Alice, offering one of her inane suggestions, asked, "Shouldn't you have a light?" In spite of my irritation with her naiveté, it struck me that a light might come in handy as I was crawling around in the dark on beams in the attic. After we got our trouble light, and I had found where the water was coming in, I came down and rushed to get the extension ladder. As I was about three rungs up the ladder, Alice came with more banal questions. Again, she asked, "What are you going to do?" With little patience, I replied, "What does it look like I am going to do? I am going up to fix the roof!" To my great consternation, she persisted with the questions, asking, "How?"

In so many instances, the solution to a problem begins with being able to ask the right question. Being the kind of person who is going to do something—even if I do not know what—I had not really thought about how I was going to repair the leak. After a couple of minutes of discussion, we were able to decide upon a temporary solution and by 11:00, we were in bed. Left to Alice's approach, we would have returned a week later to find our ceiling had caved in. Left to my approach, the least I would have done was to fall through the ceiling and the most I might have done was to fall off the roof and break both of my legs. Fortunately, in this instance, our Frenchness and Germanness was working in perfect harmony.

As the years go by a happily married couple gradually begins to develop an appreciation for the complementary nature of their differences. Although differences can continue to be sources of pain and misunderstanding, the couple learns that if they are patient with each other and stick to the task of problem solving and decision making, their differences will work for, rather than against them. For instance, the husband who fancies himself as quite a handyman, may learn that he can profit considerably from his wife who may be an accomplished seamstress. Because of her skill in laying out patterns and planning how much material she will need, she may be able to help him figure how he can get the most use out of a piece of wood.

Meeting the challenge of making differences work for rather than against them will be considerably easier if couples will, during their first year of marriage, make a special effort to become acquainted with each other and to develop the arts of simplicity and intimacy. Couples will get a feeling for how this can be accomplished if they will explore the role of television in their relationship. In fact, if either partner is addicted to television, it would help to watch another

TV addict in action. TV addicts usually are unaware of what is happening around them. When one spouse tries to talk with the other, the TV addict mumbles, "Slurp, slurp. It's third and twenty-five—wait until the commercial." It is not long before the partner has fogotten what he or she wanted to discuss. One woman who had been married for only about a year lamented that, prior to marriage, she and her husband decided to reserve intercourse for marriage. In times of temptation, she comforted herself by thinking of how nice their sex relationship would be in marriage. She particularly daydreamed about Saturday mornings when she thought they could lie in bed intertwined in each other's arms. Unfortunately, her husband was tuned to another channel. When she awakened on Saturday morning, she began to reach futilely for her husband. Then, from the living room, she heard the sound of the Saturday morning cartoons.

Although couples project in-laws to be troublesome, they often do not consider how television can interfere in their marriage. When asked if they would like to have their mother-in-law live with them during the first year of marriage, about 99.9% of engaged couples respond that, if they had a choice, they would prefer not to have anyone else living with them during that first year. This fact does not cast dispersion upon mothers-in-law or in-laws in general. In fact, in most instances, relatives and in-laws have a positive effect upon a marriage. However, if illness, or other conditions, do not make it necessary for a parent to live with a newly married couple, most prefer to take the opportunities of the first year to develop their own sense of couple identity, lifestyle, and simply to become acquainted with each other. Because television interferes much more than any mother-in-law, I suggest that a couple put aside television during the first year of their marriage. At least a mother-in-law generally sleeps at night and will not talk while her mouth is full of food. However, television goes on night and day.

A couple's effort to adjust to marriage will be considerably aided by putting aside television, tuning into each other and developing the great art of simplicity. It is generally through involvement in simple activities that couples develop the deepest sense of intimacy. It will be helpful for an engaged couple to realize that some of their most intimate moments happen while doing very simple things. The couple who enjoys walking is fortunate. When a couple is riding in a car, the one concentrating on driving may be only half there. If a couple is not unduly competitive, games like Yahtze, cards, and Backgammon can greatly facilitate their effort to develop a sense of oneness.

Considering the radical nature of this recommendation, it is surprising how many couples respond positively to the notion of setting aside television. Some will say that they considered it, but that since no one else talked about it, they thought it would be a crazy idea. However, when it was seriously viewed, the idea fit perfectly with their own pre-dispositions. Others said that although they had not previously talked about it, it made sense to set television aside. Some decided to severely limit their viewing of television by confining it to the news and some of the better-done documentaries. It may not be too extreme to suggest that the National Football League should be taken to court for alienation of affection.

It was sad to hear one fiancé exclaim, "No one is going to take my television away from me. It is all I've got." Six months later his sadly disillusioned wife lamented, "Why didn't I believe it when he said television was number one in his life? Now we have a TV set in the living room, the kitchen and even the bedroom where he insists upon intercourse during the commercials." Compare this unfortunate story with that of an engaged couple who told their parents they intended to set aside TV for the first year. Thinking that such a plan could also help their marriage, the parents also decided to set aside TV for awhile. Two months later this middle-aged father commented that he could not believe the difference it made in their marriage and family life.

INRI

*CHAPTER 8*

# Living in Faith

Other than the differences discussed in the previous chapter, there are couples who are challenged by differences in religion or denomination. The discussion of interfaith marriages involves a willingness to delve into a very sensitive subject. The sensitivity revolves around the fact that the spiritual life is deeply personal. We may believe that since religion is between "God and me," no one else need be concerned about it. I do not need to discuss it with anyone else. Since marriage is an intimate relationship, couples are encouraged to discuss the very personal subject of religion, the meaning God has to them and the way in which they intend to worship God, or if they intend to worship Him. As a marriage counselor, I am impressed with the number of very personal subjects couples are willing to discuss. Yet when couples are asked about their relationship with God, it is not unusual for someone to ask, "You're getting pretty personal, aren't you?" Religion is personal because individuals have a strong investment in the way they worship God, i.e., their denominational affiliation. They guard those affiliations.

As denominational affiliation is mentioned, it is important for couples to be clear about their own religious persuasion and that of their partner. Couples should be definite about their religious persuasion whether Christian, Jewish, Moslem, Hindu, atheist, or agnostic. If couples are members of different religions, they are, indeed, an interfaith couple. Many more engaged couples are interdenominational rather than interfaith. That is, they share the Christian faith, but are affiliated with different denominations.

Many religions and denominations are concerned about interfaith and interdenominational engagements. For instance, if a Catholic is intending to marry a person of another religion or denomination, it is necessary for the Catholic to receive a dispensation from the Catholic church. A dispensation implies that special permission is granted to enter into the marriage. The priest who is intending to witness an interfaith or interdenominational marriage, must request permission from his bishop. In requesting the permission, the priest needs to assure the bishop that he has visited with the couple and that this intended marriage will not jeopardize the faith of the Catholic party. The Catholic church believes the gift of faith is a treasured gift that should not be jeopardized.

If one simply looks at the statistics, persons entering into interfaith or interdenominational relationships tend to drift from the practice of their faith and from their denominational affiliation. The second point follows from the first. There is a far greater tendency on the part of interfaith and interdenominational couples to fail to transmit the heritage of faith to their children. The issue of transmitting the faith life is so serious that Catholics are expected to have an internalized acceptance of the decree of Vatican Council II which states:

> ...Parents must be acknowleged as the first and foremost educators of their children. Their role as religious educators is so decisive that scarcely anything can compensate for their failure in it. For it devolves on parents to create a family atmosphere so animated with love and reverence for God and

> all people that a well-rounded personal and social development will be fostered among the children. Hence, the family is the first school of those social virtues which every society needs.[10]

Since the Catholic church along with many others considers the gift of faith one of the most treasured gifts that can be transmitted to children, the bishop who serves a particular Catholic wants to be reassured that the marriage will not threaten that individual's faith or affiliation with the Catholic church.

There are some expressions of Judaism and various Christian denominations that are very concerned about interfaith and interdenominational marriages. For instance, there are Baptists who are concerned about the intention of a Baptist to marry a Catholic. The Missouri Synod Lutheran church is very concerned about interdenominational marriages. In fact, most Missouri Synod ministers would not be permitted to participate actively in the marriage of a Lutheran and a Catholic if that marriage was to be witnessed in a Catholic church. If the marriage was to be witnessed in a Missouri Synod Lutheran church, most congregations would not permit the Roman Catholic priest to participate actively in the marriage ceremony. These concerns revolve around the way in which faith may become jeopardized in an interfaith or interdenominational marriage.

Although the statistics about interfaith and interdenominational marriages are cause for pause, it is more important to examine ways in which partners can avoid becoming a fallen-away, lapsed, or unbelieving Catholic, Lutheran, Methodist, Baptist, Jew, or Muslim. It is easy to understand that a couple may feel insulted by the concern of the rabbi, minister, priest, church, or congregation about the marriage. We can understand the reason for the hesitation and take steps designed to allay the concern. The next three sections will discuss the viable alternatives from which sincere engaged couples can choose.

## Becoming One

1. Although it would be ideal for engaged couples to become members of the same religion or denomination, that is a difficult idea to implement. Some emphasis is placed upon this recommendation because of the way in which faith-life is affected in the interfaith or interdenominational marriage. For me as a Catholic, it is extremely difficult to insist upon this recommendation. If I were to do so, there are Catholics who would say, "Well, my affiliation is not all that strong, but my fiancée's Lutheran affiliation is very strong. Thus, it would seem to make more sense for me to become Lutheran." Because I am very grateful for all this religion has meant to me and for the role of the Catholic church in the world, I am reluctant to encourage a Catholic, even though loosely affiliated, to walk away from the church.

On the other hand, I do not want to offend persons of other denominations. I do not want to imply, "It is important to be members of the same denomination, and since we do not want Catholics to walk away from the church, it will be perfectly all right for members of other denominations and religious groups to become Catholic."

Although it is beneficial to be members of the same religion or denomination, it is very difficult to determine how to implement this recommendation. It is perhaps most easily implemented by those who have not had, or have only had a weak religious or denominational affiliation. Yet they may have been attracted to religion and may have yearned for a more profound religious experience. It is important not to "change for the other," or simply to keep the peace or to please future in-laws. One should not simply change to the other's religion or denomination as a way of resolving a family squabble or to do something that would be nicey-nice.

The request for membership in a particular religion or denomination must be prompted by deeply internalized convictions regarding the truths of that religion and by a strong desire to live by the truths enunciated by the religion. The step into membership must be prompted by a conviction that such a step will be a significant aid to one's goal of realizing the beatific vision—to meet God face-to-face.

Because the Catholic church is concerned about one partner becoming Catholic just to please the other partner, couples have complained that they felt the priest was discouraging them from becoming Catholic. Of course, the priest is simply discouraging them from making a change prior to the wedding to be certain that they really want to change and are not just changing to please the other or to make it a nicey-nice wedding.

Although choosing a third denomination is ill-advised, this is sometimes done by those involved in a power struggle. If a Catholic and a Lutheran do not want to remain interdenominational, yet neither feels able to change to the denomination of the other, they may think it quite reasonable to become Episcopalian. Religion may be one of the many ways in which the power struggle is manifested. It seems as if they are saying, "Well, I don't want you and your parents to win, so we will just become members of a third denomination." When couples choose a denomination for this reason, the matter of denominational affiliation appears not to mean much to either of the partners. Because those with strong religious ties and denominational affiliation become better candidates for marriage than are those who are indifferent, the phenomenon of loose affiliation with religion is lamentable.

## Maintaining a Strong Affiliation With Different Religions or Denominations

2. The second viable alternative is for the couple to retain their interfaith or interdenominational status. That is, they would remain affiliated with their own religion or denomination. If this is to be effective, it will be important for each individual to become actively affiliated with his/her own denomination or religion.

Some may be concerned that strong affiliation will open the door to intensification of the differences and to increased conflict. There is the temptation to think that there will be less hassle if only one of the partners is strongly affiliated and if the other one is loosely affiliated.

In fact, experience shows the opposite to be true. Some of the most deeply bigoted and prejudiced people are those who are ill-informed about religion and who have a loose or non-existent affiliation with a religion or denomination. These are the individuals who, invariably, preface their criticisms, "I don't know much about religion, but I do know that you Catholics give blind and stupid obedience to the Pope." Or the person may criticize, "...I do know the Baptists are a bunch of rigidly narrow-minded fundamentalists who have no appreciation for intellectual pursuit."

It makes no sense to stress the importance of religion as the basic fabric of the marriage and then to say, "...but if you aren't Catholic, we really hope you aren't anything else or that you are weak in whatever you happen to be." People with the strongest affiliation have the greatest appreciation for the fact that others may also be strong in their affiliation. Of course, this is assuming that the strength of affiliation is not based upon blind prejudice towards other groups. Some individuals may not so much be Jewish, Catholic, Baptist or Lutheran as they may be anti-everything else. These are often the relatively closed-minded people who appear to think everyone else is destined to hell.

Yet it must be recognized that a strong affiliation on the part of each partner does not necessarily reduce the pain of the interdenominational marriage. Some of the greatest pain is experienced by those couples in which one is Roman Catholic and the other is a member of a denomination or religious group such as the Missouri Synod Lutheran church. The dynamics of a blend such as this explains some of the pain that is involved.

In many instances, both the Missouri Synod Lutheran and the Roman Catholic also have a culturally-oriented affiliation. That is, the Roman Catholic may be tied to an ethnic group such as the Italian or Irish. On the other hand, the Missouri Synod Lutheran may be strongly tied to a German background. Along with this, their individual homes were probably looked upon as domestic churches in which the faith-life was actively imparted to each of them. Prayer and devotions may have been an integral part of their family life. The family may have attended church together and been actively involved in church activities. For many of these couples, the church was the center of their social, cultural and faith-life. In addition to this, each of them may have attended parochial schools and church-related colleges.

Each of these persons may have a deep regard for the strength of the other's affiliation and yet feel very bad that they are affiliated with different denominations. It is because their own religion is so important to them, that they yearn to share denominational affiliation. Before further consideration of this second alternative, it is helpful to recognize a third alternative.

## Deciding Not to Marry

3. Although this third alternative sounds frightening, deciding not to marry must be acknowledged. This is the recognition that the nature of the religious or denominational difference is such that the couples should not continue their engagement. It takes a great deal of courage for conscientious couples to explore this alternative. Perhaps many couples do not seriously consider this alternative because religion is frequently not discussed until the relationship has become considerably advanced, committed, and serious.

Although there are several explanations for the phenomenon, it is somewhat unfortunate that people do not view their religious or denominational affiliation with the kind of seriousness that would lead them away from serious involvement with someone who did not share the same religion or denominational affiliation. On the other hand, it is inspiring to meet the occasional couple who have decided, before becoming engaged, to resolve satisfactorily the religious issue. Meaningful ecumenical dialogue is not facilitated by those who either minimize or exaggerate differences. Instead, it is aided by those who have deep personal convictions, strong ties and an openness to dialogue with those of other beliefs. Although it can sound a little harsh, some interfaith couples may need to consider that their greatest handicap may be that "religion has never been that big of a deal." In saying this, it must also be recognized that some same-faith or same denomination couples are "just happening" to marry someone of the same faith or denomination. It may not have been that they placed so much emphasis upon marrying someone who shared their faith. Instead the sameness may have resulted more from coincidence than actual intention.

## Interdenominational Marriages

Denominational affiliations may be so important to some couples that they would break off an engagement. Yet there are ways in which committed couples can live interdenominationally. If couples choose to retain their interfaith or interdenominational status, it will be important for them to accentuate the issues upon which they agree. Although it is patronizing and ineffective to sweep differences under the rug, the couples will have to build upon that which they agree while learning to deal effectively with the areas of disagreement. The following exercise may help couples to identify vital areas of agreement. Acknowledge whether or not each of you agrees or disagrees with each statement listed below:

| Woman | | Man |
|---|---|---|
| A D | | A D |
| | I believe in God the Father almighty, | |
| | Creator of Heaven and earth | |
| | And in Jesus Christ | |
| | His only Son our Lord. | |
| | Who was conceived by the Holy Spirit | |
| | Born of the Virgin Mary | |
| | Suffered under Pontius Pilate | |
| | Was crucified | |
| | Died | |
| | And was buried. | |
| | He descended into Hell | |
| | On the third day he arose again from the dead, | |
| | He ascended into Heaven | |
| | And sitteth at the right hand of the Father almighty. | |
| | From thence He shall come to judge the living and the dead. | |
| | I believe in the Holy Spirit | |

The holy catholic church
The communion of saints
The forgiveness of sins,
The resurrection of the body
And life everlasting.

If each of you is a Christian, it is quite likely that you have immediately identified these statements as the Apostle's Creed. Examine the statements with which you both agreed, those on which you both disagreed, and those on which one of you disagreed. It is quite likely that you agreed with all of the statements. The Apostle's Creed is common to most Christian denominations and it is generally recognized as the bottom line for believing Christians. That is, these statements are the minimal belief system for an individual referring to him or herself as Christian. Some of you may have had difficulty agreeing with the statement, "Holy catholic church." However, that phrase is used by many denominations and denotes the universal church and not the Roman Catholic with a capital "C."

If you agreed with those statements, you will have a common belief system upon which you can build your religious practices. To the extent to which you disagreed with each other about the statements, your efforts to establish a spiritual union will be complicated.

If couples intend to retain their interdenominational status, it is essential to attend inquiry classes in each other's denominations. Even if you would not want to join that denomination, it is important that you understand and respect the beliefs of your partner's denomination. It is quite likely that the Catholic party will learn a great deal about the Catholic faith from an inquiry class and that the other person will learn a great deal about their own denomination when they attend an inquiry class for that denomination. If it is at all possible, couples should attend the inquiry classes together.

Along with all the other discussion you will be having about the impact of being an interdenominational or interfaith couple, it will help to list the questions you have about each other's denomination. Although these questions may be discussed during an inquiry class, raise them with the priest and minister with whom you are working.

It is because of the need to accentuate and build upon the issues on which they agree, that interdenominational and interfaith couples find many priests discourage them from pronouncing their marriage vows during the celebration of the Mass. Since the Eucharist is intrinsic to the celebration of the Mass and since that remains an area of disagreement between Christian denominations, many think it ill-advised to begin the wedding day by highlighting an area of disagreement.

Although it is possible to plan a meaningful wedding liturgy, Mass is so important to most Catholics that it is difficult for them to think of being married without integrating it with the Sacrament of the Eucharist. This can be especially difficult for parents of the Catholic partner. One father was angry that the priest discouraged his daughter, who was marrying a Lutheran, from having the celebration of the Mass. He protested that his daughter was marrying an extremely fine Lutheran man and that he was insulted by the priest's prejudice towards interdenominational couples. However, he needed to examine his own prejudice to realize that he was shoving down the throat of his future son-in-law a part of the Catholic belief system that was not accepted by his son-in-law and his family. Not celebrating the Liturgy of the Eucharist may be a common courtesy extended to one's non-Catholic partner and his or her family. It may be the beginning of helping them to understand the kinds of adaptations and adjustments they need to make to each other's beliefs.

The discussion of the Mass, as part of the wedding ceremony, also calls attention to the question of Eucharistic hospitality. There are some who are offended by the expectation of the Catholic Church that those of other denominations will not partake in the Eucharist. Of course, people of other denominations are invited to participate in the rest of the Mass and other services that are part of the Catholic faith. However, because of the unique and particular meaning of the Eucharist, usually those who are not Catholic do not receive Communion. Catholics believe that the Eucharist is the Body and Blood of Christ, and that those receiving the Eucharist are in communion (common-union) with the Holy Father. There are many people of other denominations who do not believe in the real presence, and it is a rare exception for a member of another denomination to accept the spiritual leadership of the Holy Father—the Roman Pontiff. If one views the stance of the Catholic church in light of its integrity, it is courteous for others to respect those beliefs.

When an interdenominational couple is worshiping together in the Catholic church, they may want to consider various ways of acknowledging the request of the Catholic church. The non-Catholic may remain in his or her place while his or her partner goes to Communion. While waiting in place, he or she could pray that all denominations will be united. While the non-Catholic partner remains in his or her place, he or she serves as a sign of the separation between the denominations and reminds us of the need to unite all Christian denominations.

An alternative approach is for the non-Catholic partner to approach Communion with his or her partner, and to ask the priest to pray with them for unity. Since many Eucharistic ministers may be unaware of this practice, it may be best for the interdenominational couple to approach the priest (as distinct from the lay Eucharistic minister) for Communion, a blessing and a prayer for unity. Facing the differences between the denominations may do much more to bring about reconciliation than sweeping the differences under the rug and walking around oblivious to problems which cry for resolution.

To promote common understanding, it may be advisable for couples to discuss the religious practices that were common in their individual homes. Consider whether there were family devotions, scriptural reading, prayer at meal-time, religious magazines and books. Did the family gather together for evening prayer? A discussion of the practices that were common in each of the homes can lead to a consideration of the practices a couple intends to integrate into their own conjugal family life.

The interdenominational couple is challenged to blend and integrate those beliefs, practices and customs which are easily integrated. Other than using certain spontaneous prayers for meal grace, the partners may at times use the meal grace common to Catholics and at other times use that which is common to that of the other denomination. When the Our Father is prayed, the couple could conclude it, "For Thine is the Kingdom and the power and the glory now and forever."

Engaged and married couples should be involved in each other's parish or congregation. They should attend the social and educational programs and should be willing to serve on various committees in each other's parish or congregation. They are expected to support financially each of their churches to the best of their means.

Planning the wedding ceremony in cooperation with their respective pastors is an excellent way for the couple to understand both their common and their different approaches to worship and prayer. This ceremony can serve as a witness to the faith-life of the interfaith or interdenominational couple. Depending upon local customs and denominational practices, it is possible that both a priest and minister could be present for the wedding. In most instances, the pastor of the host parish or congregation functions as the celebrant who receives the vows while the guest cleric may add a blessing, a prayer or some appropriate words at the end of the ceremony. In some instances, the guest priest or minister may prefer to sit with the congregation.

## Children

No discussion of interfaith and interdenominational marriages can be complete without a discussion of the way in which children affect the interdenominational or interfaith couple. The discussion of interfaith or interdenominational marriages often proceeds rather smoothly until one approaches the issue of the children's religion. Since religion is so personal and so important, it is understandable that each of the partners wants to share with the children that which has been so very important to them. As Alice and I reflect upon our life as parents, we realize that transmission of the faith has been the most vital gift we have given our children. We also know that our faith has provided us with an opportunity to relate on an extremely intimate level. Although the Frenchness and Germanness may drive us up a tree, the common faith-life broadens our perspective, strengthens our souls and psyches, and provides us with a common goal.

It is frequently not until couples begin to discuss the denominational affiliation for the children that they begin to realize how important their own denominational affiliation is to them. It is generally agreed that it is advisable to bring up children to be members of only one denomination. There are those who say in a misguided and unrealistic effort to avoid shoving religion down the throat of their children that they will wait to present religion and denomination to them until they are sixteen or eighteen and capable of making their own choices. This shortsighted approach denies the value of religion. If individuals of that mentality are to be consistent with themselves, they will need to delay formal education of their sons and daughters until the children are capable of deciding whether or not they want to learn to read, write and do figures.

Some engaged couples explain that they will bring up their children to be Christian. That is, they will simply expose them to the various denominations, have them participate rather actively in each of their denominations and bring them up to realize that they are bi- multi- or non-denominational. Although this approach sounds relatively harmonious, it overlooks a number of realities.

One of the basic reasons children should be brought up as a member of a single denomination is that children do not cope well with ambiguities. They do much better when there is consistency in the presentation of values and worship. As much as young children want the same story told to them in the same way, they benefit most if religion is presented in a consistent fashion. This does not mean that they would not learn about the denomination of the other spouse and that they should never go to the church of the other parent. They should come to know that going to the church of the other parent is something that they do on very special days or at special times when they are being visited by their grandparents.

This brings us to the delicate matter of the denomination in which the children are going to be raised. In turn, this question brings us face-to-face with the promise the Catholic party is asked to make. Although these promises have been modified since the 1960's, they continue to be a source of heartache for some interdenominational couples. Sensitive Catholics regret the hurt that was caused to members of other denominations who felt they were coerced into promising to rear their children Catholic. Of course, there is deep regret for the fact that interdenominational and interfaith couples were denied a church wedding. In an effort to discourage interfaith marriages, a sense of being a second class church member was conveyed to those entering "mixed marriages."

Although the non-Catholic party is no longer expected to sign or make any of the promises, it must be recognized that a Catholic cannot make promises that his fiancé or fiancée is unaware of, or which cannot be coped with. The Catholic party is asked to promise that he or she reaffirms his/her faith in Jesus Christ and that he or she intends to continue living that faith in the Catholic church. Since the Catholic party to the marriage is asking that his/her marriage be recognized not only as a legal contract but as a sacrament of the Church, it follows that the Catholic party intends to continue membership in the Catholic church. Lacking such intent, the sacramental aspect of the marriage is irrelevant. Next the Catholic party is asked to respect the faith of his or her partner. However, most objection is raised because the Catholic party is also expected to promise to do all in his or her power to share the faith with their children by having them baptized and educated as Catholics. It is frequently the Catholic party who objects most vociferously to this expectation of the Catholic church. Spirited discussions about this expectation convinces me that very early in their relationship engaged couples should become intimately aware of these promises and their implications. Of course, the promises stem from a belief that anyone committed to an idea, principle or faith wants to share it with others.

Some object that this promise contradicts the concept of respect for the conscience of their partner. Others object that the promise is motivated by a fear of survival. Others complain that the policy of the Catholic church should be like that of most other denominations that do not expect these promises. Some maintain that the establishment of the promises stems from an elitist position prompting the Catholic church to treat other religions and denominations as "second-rate." Some individuals whose parents are interfaith complain that they were given the impression that the religion of the non-Catholic parent was inferior. Frequently, this complaint only makes the church a scapegoat. Closer examination often reveals that the non-Catholic parent's loose association with his/her church was a more relevant contributor to the perception of being "second-class." One fiancé explained that he overheard his ten-year-old nephew complain that he wanted to quit the Catholic church and join his father's congregation. When asked the reason for this, he explained: "Catholics are always going to church. Dad hardly ever goes and I don't want to go to church so much."

## Why the Promises?

There is rationale in the Catholic church's position that the Catholic party makes certain promises. The Catholic church teaches that all Christian denominations teach and uphold the faith which God sent to humankind through His son, Jesus Christ. However, as various groups separated themselves from the original single Christian community, united under one visible head, the Pope, there was no longer a unity among Christian people. Separation from this Catholic communion brought about the loss of both the sign and the reality of oneness.

We all believe our church to be the true church. The Catholic church believes that she has retained, most consistently and most fully, the totality of the truths taught by Jesus Christ, and that the most complete spiritual life is to be found under the umbrella of and within the Catholic church. She does believe that the offices of the papacy and the bishops in union with him have been designated by Christ to be the visible sign of his presence and teaching authority on earth.

Although it is understandable that one may disagree with the premise of the Catholic church, it is unfair for couples to place the entire burden for resolving the dilemma upon the churches. Some argue, "Since the differences between the churches are causing us problems, the churches ought to get their act together, resolve their problems and quit complicating our lives." Although the separation between the denominations is a contradiction, it is unrealistic and shortsighted to place all the burden for resolution upon the institutional churches. After all, churches are only structures for groups of individuals. Couples must also see how they can be a small part of the solution rather than part of the problem. Certain cavalier couples simply sign the promises with no understanding of their meaning and no intention of following them.

Rather than to rear their children in one denomination or the other, some couples maintain that they will raise them to be Christian. Although this is another resolution which sounds reconciliatory, in reality, it does not accomplish much. Those who pride themselves on their nondenominational Christianity need to appreciate that nondenominationalism is actually a denomination.

Unfortunate as is the separation between the churches, little is accomplished by denying the fact of the separation and by failing to participate in the effort to resolve the problems and issues separating the churches. As long as the separation continues, people will have to make choices about their affiliation and that of their children.

It will be helpful for interfaith couples to look upon the promises as an opportunity for fruitful discussion rather than as an obstacle to be overcome. If a Protestant party were marrying a member of another Protestant denomination in an interfaith marriage, there would be no promises required in most instances. Neither would there be the challenge to "clear the air" over this important issue of the religious denomination of any children to be born. An issue as sensitive as this is best dealt with, painful as such confrontation may be, before the marriage commitment. Prior to marriage, each can still go his or her own way; that option is removed by marriage. The innocent offspring then becomes the brunt of friction that mother and father have not satisfactorily resolved. A common experience among other interdenominational couples is that they seldom face the need to discuss the impact of their "interdenominationalness." Thus after some five years of marriage, they may explain that they have drifted away from any meaningful affiliation with their denomination or any meaningful practice of their faith. A Lutheran may say, "Yes, I was very active in Luther League and my religion meant a good deal to me. However, we didn't want to go to different churches. I tried her Baptist Church on a couple of occasions and was horribly embarrassed. Do you realize that if you want to become a Baptist, you have to stand up in front of the entire congregation and ask to be received into the congregation? I would die before I would do anything like that. I also found them to be terribly fundamental."

The Baptist spouse may respond, "No, I didn't want to be going off to church by myself so I tried the Lutheran church a couple of times. But I was so turned off. Do you realize that their ministers wear collars just like priests and that they even wear some kind of vestments? I thought I was in a Catholic church. I was terribly confused. Yes, my religion had been very important to me. In fact, my father was a minister and I went to a Baptist college. But now it has just kind of floated away."

They may go on to explain that when their children were born, they avoided the issue of religion because they did not want to get into the sensitive subject of infant versus adult baptism. When persons of other than Catholic denominations plan to marry Catholics, they will be asked to explore thoroughly this issue of denominational affiliation for the children.

However, the meaning of the promises has not yet been faced. A close reading of the final promise essentially states that the Catholic party will do all in his/her power to transmit the faith to the children by having them baptized and educated as Catholics. Just what does, "All in my power" mean? This question must be thoroughly discussed with the priest who is working with a couple. There are those who say, "The promise means exactly what it says, "The children will be raised Catholic." There are others who place emphasis upon the "all in my power" dimension. They ask the Catholic partner to assess the meaning of all in my power. The term "all in my power" is frequently thought to mean that the Catholic party honestly intends the children to be Catholic, that the children will be raised as Catholics, and that the Catholic partner is affirmed in that belief. It is understandable that either one of the couple who is deeply committed to his/her own denomination would want the children to be reared as members of that denomination. In order to gain an understanding of how this difficult issue applies to a couple, it is advisable to consult the priest serving a particular couple or with the Chancery office of the diocese in which they are to be married.

Although there are those who become angry about these promises, the reality is that the church is asking engaged couples to come to grips with a very serious issue. Even if the promises are thrown out the window, a couple is still faced with making a decision about the matter of denominational affiliation for their children. It must also be remembered that no one is demanding that anyone remain Catholic, nor is anyone threatened with hell if they do not have their marriage approved by or witnessed by the Catholic church. Yet it must also be remembered that Catholics are not accustomed to talking about the freedom of people to leave the Catholic church. The church itself operates upon the assumption that once a person believes in the Catholic church, it is difficult to understand how they could in good conscience leave the church. Most certainly, the conscience of each of the parties to the marriage must be respected. However it is also true that the Catholic church and her leadership must follow its conscience. Couples are asked to take an adult look at critical issues, to make an adult decision, and to accept the consequences of their decision. As much as one may not want to be faced with the rules, regulations and expectations of the Catholic church, the teaching authority of the church does not permit individual members to dictate the conditions for membership.

One couple explained that they made the decision about denominational affiliation for their children prior to their marriage. The wife explained that it was difficult for her to not have the children baptized and educated in her denomination. However, she explained that they found ways in which they could worship and grow spiritually as a family. She took instructions in the Catholic faith before they were married and again before they had their first child. She thought it was important to know as much about each other's faith as possible and to respect each other's beliefs. They explained that to disagree on one point does not mean that one is wrong and the other is right. They were exposed to many different teachings within their denominations as well as other sources and decided what teachings each would follow. They frequently discussed theology and realized that each had to answer for his/her own decision and, therefore, did not feel a need to establish "right" and "wrong" when there were differences.

They remained active in their respective churches and at the same time did what they could in each other's church, that is, teaching in the preschool of religion when the children were young, and attending Bible study together. They attended interdenominational seminars as a couple and as a family. For six years they attended a Christian Family Camp and attended several retreats. Family devotions were a regular part of their family life. As young adults, their children remained Catholic, but they also felt comfortable in the Protestant church. There did not seem to be any confusion as they were growing up as to why their Mom went to a different church. They attended services together on many occasions such as on Christmas Eve, or Easter Vigil and Easter morning.

They thought it was presumptious to leave the decision about the children's denominational affiliation until the children were born. They did not think the decision should be made by young children. They did not think a promise should be made to raise the children Catholic if there was no intention to do so.

They believed their interfaith marriage worked well, not because of any set prescription, but because of their basic temperaments. They were able to tolerate a lot of give and take without keeping score. They disagreed openly on most everything in twenty-eight years of marriage—except religious affiliation. That was decided before marriage.

[10] Abbott, Walter M., ed. *The Documents of Vatican II*. "Declaration on Christian Education," New York: Guild Press, 1966, p.641.

*CHAPTER 9*

# Money Matters

Having already discussed the importance of want management, it is essential to consider some principles for effective money management. Each person brings to marriage a personal financial agenda: a value system, attitudes, assets, and liabilities. Values are already formed and are deeply ingrained in us prior to marriage. They have been greatly influenced by parents, how we were raised, and where we have lived. The value of what we consider good and desirable is in part associated with money as a measure of success and personal fulfillment. Consequently, our attitudes affect how we view and manage money. Individuals may not completely understand themselves or their partner. It is important to talk openly about values related to money. There may be differences you are unaware of or have chosen to ignore. The bringing of "you" and "me" to "us" does not happen automatically.

Along with our values, we bring assets and liabilities, the savings and debts of each partner. You are sharing in a commitment of which you have had no control. This commitment for better or worse, affects your life style. You are caught up with financial obligations "after the fact." Many couples are concerned with the whirlwind of expenses of a wedding, honeymoon, furnishing an apartment, and adjustments to their new status. Depending upon the seriousness of the situation, the degree of anxiety and frustration varies from a gnawing uneasiness to emotional displays of anger, resentment, and power struggles. Time and energy are spent in futile worry and arguments. It is important to examine sound principles of money management.

The purpose of money management is to utilize to the maximum your financial resources. It allows you to make choices and to set priorities in order to meet your unique needs and wants. Sound management reduces anxiety and frustration. It leads to fulfillment and security as you learn to live within your income and reach financial goals. Money management is a process by which you control your money rather than having it control you.

Assuming that the average couple has forty years to work, accounting for inflation (even a modest rate) and the possibility of two incomes, it is likely that you will earn more than a million dollars. How often have you said, "If only I had a million...?" Yet you have the potential to control more than a million dollars. As that thought sinks in, we begin to appreciate the challenge to manage that money to the best of our ability in order to ensure the well-being of our family and to share with others for the common good. How tragic it must be to come to what should be one's golden years of retirement only to realize that for endless years we have worked for our money rather than having our money work for us.

Our chance of meeting the challenge will be improved if we use the model of the American free enterprise system. Specifically, the business partnership is an excellent example. The marriage is a legal partnership. Like the business partnership, the couple can set goals, budget, borrow, invest, spend, and even go bankrupt. Financially successful marriages, like successful businesses, follow an orderly procedure. In other words, the system is the answer. The remainder of this chapter will concentrate on four aspects of successful money management: budgeting, borrowing, savings, and spending.

An essential first step to successful budgeting is goal setting. A budget is worthless unless it helps you meet your goals. Your values will now be put into specific needs and wants. You will ask, "What is important to us?" Priorities should be established and placed on an ongoing time frame. Goals make you aware of the ways you need to develop, use and control your financial resources. It is important that both partners provide input. If your ways of achieving goals are incompatible and inconsistent, conflict will begin.

First, write your individual goals separately. Divide them into three categories: short-term (first year), intermediate (two to five years), and long-term (six years to retirement). List three or four goals for each category. Put an estimated dollar amount after each goal and a date by which the goal is to be achieved. Share your list with each other discussing the common as well as the different goals. Together negotiate, compromise, and find solutions. This process will help you establish the goals for your partnership. These goals will form the foundation for your financial planning. They should be reviewed at least annually, and they may be altered to meet your changing needs.

You would never consider building a house without a blueprint or driving across the country without a map. Yet most people embark on life's journey, expending their million plus dollars of earning power without a guide. A budget is a written plan of your plans and priorities for saving and spending. The key phrase is "before you spend." It allows you to look at alternatives before you make a financial commitment. It forces you to look at the reality of your situation. This is most important when making decisions on large ticket items such as housing, automobiles, furniture, and vacations. Planning before you spend may cause you to avoid following an unduly materialistic life style which could easily become a millstone around your neck. Many marriages are destroyed because of the tensions caused by the debts spirating from the life-style in which some couples become ensnared.

Your budget helps you watch and adjust expenditures to guarantee achievement of your goals. The importance of your written goals takes on special meaning. The budget provides time to make emergency adjustments and the chance to get back on track. Lastly, the budget helps you to see the overall financial growth (net worth) of your partnership.

There are numerous examples of excellent budget guides. One highly recommended booklet is *Money Management—Your Financial Plan.* This helpful booklet contributed significantly to the ideas developed in this chapter. To begin your budget you need to know your income, expenses, and net worth. Keep your account simple but real. Round off numbers and estimate where figures are unknown. If you receive income on a regular basis, it is easier to use twelve-month planning periods. The yearly plan also allows time for adjustments due to emergencies or other variables.

On a worksheet, list joint monthly take-home pay and any other spendable income that you can regularly expect. Be accurate. Do not count expected raises or bonuses until they are actually received. If income is based on commissions or seasonal employment, you must estimate conservatively using figures from past years. The dual income family needs to decide carefully whether or not to plan regular living expenditures on both incomes. It is generally advised not to become dependent upon two incomes for day-to-day expenses. Serious financial difficulty can arise if one income should cease due to illness, unemployment, child-rearing or other considerations. The "second income" can be an excellent source of revenue to build an emergency fund, start a down payment on a home, pay off debts, or begin an investment program.

List your fixed, flexible and periodic expenses on another worksheet. To help you with estimates for the different categories, look at present bills and records of the past year. Begin a record of present spending in order to develop a clearer picture of spending habits.

Fixed expenses are those you have promised to pay regularly whether monthly, quarterly, or yearly. Examples are: rent or mortgage payments, taxes, utilities, insurance premiums, installment payments, educational fees, transportation, personal allowances, membership dues, contributions, savings and subscriptions. Savings are considered a fixed expense. Savings should consist of an emergency fund and savings for goals and long-term investment. It is generally advisable to have three to six month's net pay placed in reserve to meet unexpected expenses such as major auto or appliance repair, illness or unemployment. This fund should be replenished regularly. It is important that some money be allocated for personal allowances to be used as each individual wishes. This is especially important in the case of an unemployed partner. Children should also receive allowances.

Flexible expenses are those which may or may not occur monthly and vary in amount. Included are: food, clothing, household equipment, home improvement, household help, gifts, transportation, health care, personal care, contributions, entertainment, and other miscellaneous items. It is easier to adjust or eliminate items in flexible expenses because they do not involve already committed obligations.

There are some fixed and flexible expenses which occur periodically, such as insurance premiums, tuition, holiday gifts, or major clothing purchases. Usually these are large amounts which are difficult to take from one paycheck. Make a list of periodic expenses, date due, and total amount needed. Divide by the twelve planning periods. That amount should be set aside each period in order to make payment when due. It is helpful to place this money in a separate savings account earmarked "periodic expenses." Besides keeping it safe until needed, it will be earning interest for you. Your money will be working for you! This periodic account is essential for a healthy cash flow. It may take some discipline to begin, but once accomplished, it can become painless.

You are now ready to balance your total expense against your income. Do you have a surplus? Are the expenditures greater? Do not be discouraged if you are over your budget on your first attempt. Remember you have not spent a cent—you are just planning! You now have a clearer picture of your spending pattern. This is the time to analyze your budget. Obviously, if you have a minus balance, you will need to make cuts. Ask the question, "Do we really need this?" Make trade-offs, look at your priorities. Will you achieve goals with this plan? Check if certain categories are out of proportion. You may be surprised by how much you have been spending on certain items, such as lunches, clothing, transportation. You may note that you have not provided for upcoming known expenses. After making adjustments, try your plan for a few months. Be open to making necessary adjustments and changes. Your budget is unique. Its main purpose is to help you achieve your goals and to make your money work for you.

The management of your finances is a joint effort. Successful partnerships in both business and marriage maximize strengths and minimize weaknesses. To begin with, the partner more suited to record keeping might take the initiative in collecting data. However, it is strongly recommended that both partners accept responsibility for the implementation of the budget. It is imperative that each clearly understands his/her area of responsibility. Specific time, preferably twice a month, ought to be set aside to pay bills, to keep records, and to talk over financial concerns. Regular and sincere discussions with mutual decisions can "nip" many a problem in the bud. Managing your money can be fun as you accept the challenge to learn, plan and work together.

Evaluation is necessary if goals are to be met. With the budget in place and operating, the next step is to take your financial temperature. This is done through preparing a net worth statement. The net worth statement is a list of your assets (what you own) and liabilities (what you owe) balanced at a specific point in time. The statement should be prepared at the beginning of your partnership and updated annually. This procedure will help you see if you are meeting your goals. It can point out areas where change can be made and offer direction for future planning. Once again we refer you to *Money Management —Your Financial Plan* for a form and further information to help you prepare your net worth statement.

One of the major decisions facing a couple is the use of credit. To borrow or not to borrow becomes the question. The average engaged couple has been raised in the aftermath of middle class America's ability to buy and enjoy the products of advanced technology. The phenomenon of consumer credit—the ability to buy now and pay later—injects life in the economy, raises the standard of living, and opens the doors to new avenues of satisfying needs and wants whether they be economic, enrichment, or sheer enjoyment. This trust in the consumer has worked well over the years. However, as outstanding customer debt rose from $21.5 billion in 1950 to over

$450 billion in 1984, there is certainly reason for concern. In spite of the uncertainty of inflation or recession, the astronomical federal debt, and the rise in personal bankruptcy, America's love affair with credit is very much alive. The advertising industry bombards us with subtle, and not so subtle messages that you not only deserve the best, but you should have it now. Stores and lending institutions vie for your acceptance of their little "plastic" cards with enticing credit lines and varied payment plans. Having become accustomed to the lifestyle provided by your parents, it is no wonder that you want to begin married life where they are leaving off. As you review your needs and wants, there is the danger of seeing credit as an extension of your income or another form of cash instead of debt.

Consumer credit is using someone else's money to buy goods or services now with a promise to pay back out of future income. For this you agree to fixed payments including a finance and/or interest charge. There are three basic types of credit accounts:

*Regular or 30-day charge account.* This is a convenient way to handle regular purchases or services where you promise to pay in full within ten to thirty days after the billing date. There is usually no finance charge if paid by the specific time.

*Revolving or open-ended account.* This type of account usually has a limited line of credit. It can be used repeatedly for purchases up to the set limit of credit. It can either be paid in full when billed or you may choose to pay an agreed portion of the balance. Finance charges are usually assessed on the unpaid balance.

*Installment credit loan.* This is an agreement for a specific amount, usually repaid in equal installments over a specified period of time. It often requires a down payment. Finance charges may vary depending upon the amount of the loan, time to be repaid, and whether or not collateral is provided. Installment credit is used for high priced purchases such as automobiles, home improvements, or education costs.

Before using credit, it is necessary to understand its pros and cons and to analyze carefully its impact upon your financial situation. Used wisely, credit provides the advantage of using goods and services while you are paying for them. Costly items such as automobiles, home improvements or further education can be more quickly attained through a careful plan. A financial emergency can be temporarily handled through credit. With the use of credit cards, you can shop or travel without carrying large sums of money. You have the option of making one payment for a number of purchases. You have a record of expenses. Stores often give credit customers advance notice of sales and the convenience of shopping by telephone.

One of the greatest disadvantages of credit buying is the effect it has upon your future income. Choices and alternatives become less flexible as this income is committed to repayment of debt. Unknowns regarding inflation, unemployment, and salary increases can gravely affect your ability to meet every day expenses, let alone indebtedness. The cost of credit needs to be considered. You are paying for the privilege of extended payments which usually makes purchases more costly than if paying cash. The relative ease in obtaining and using credit may cause overspending and the "debt trap." You run the risk of repossession of purchases, loss of collateral or garnishment of wages if unable to meet payments in time.

Is credit for you? Your question can best be answered by looking at your needs and the options available to you. Is it possible to save for purchases? Are you willing to wait or use savings for major purchases? Is the need or want worth going into debt?

How much credit can you safely consider? Your working budget will be your best guide. Although there are "rules of thumb" to follow, the ability to borrow safely will depend upon the relationship of all debt to your total net income. A general guideline is not to owe more than 15 or 20% of your take home pay, not including mortgage payments. Another good rule is not to owe more than you can pay in eighteen to twenty-four months. It is important to be aware of your debt ratio at all times.

Some warning signals of excessive debt are:

—Spending more than 20% of your take-home pay on monthly installments, not including mortgage payments.

—Becoming late in paying bills or juggling payments to your creditors.

—Using your credit card to borrow cash to meet ordinary expenses.

—Finding it impossible to save.

—Taking out a debt consolidation loan.

—Being telephoned by bill collectors for collection agencies.

—Being worried about debt.

If you find that you have overextended your credit, you will need to develop a plan to cut expenses and pay off your debt. Going cold turkey may be the only answer. Promise each other not to add any new debt for at least a year. Do not use your credit cards. If they are tempting you, put them in a safety deposit box, give them to someone to keep for you, or destroy them. Review your budget, eliminating or cutting down on all unnecessary expenses. Put aside any extra money to reduce your debt. With perseverance and patience, you can learn to control your money rather than to have it control you.

If serious financial difficulties cannot be resolved, it may be necessary to seek the help of a credit counseling service. There are non-profit organizations such as Consumer Credit Counselors, who help overextended debtors develop a plan to repay creditors. There is often no charge, or only a small fee for this service. Check with the Better Business Bureau, Chamber of Commerce, the National Foundation of Consumer Credit, or various social agencies for a non-profit counseling service in your area. You may want to make this contact:

National Foundation of Consumer Credit
Suite 601
8701 Georgia Avenue
Silver Spring, MD 20910

Some ways to prevent getting into trouble with debt are:

—*Plan* credit purchases using your budget and the ratio of debt to total income as a guide.

—Remember debt is a fixed expense. It must be paid.

—Do not use credit cards to borrow cash.

—Do not use credit for items that will be used up or lose value before they are paid for.

—Control impulse buying. Do not buy anything on credit that you would not pay cash for.

—Keep the number of credit cards to a minimum. Two or three are more than sufficient.

—Do not carry credit cards on a regular basis, especially if you are an impulse spender.

—Shop for credit. Finance/interest charges vary. Check for interest free 30-60-90 day plans. Know the true cost of credit and the annual percentage rate (APR).

A number of consumer credit laws have been enacted to inform and protect you. Copies of these laws can be obtained from your public library, Credit Bureau, or government information centers. Some of these laws are:

*Truth in Lending.* Requires lenders to provide certain information *before* credit is given, especially the dollar amount and annual percentage rate (APR) of finance charges.

*Fair Credit Reporting Act.* Protects your right to know what consumer information has been reported to the Credit Bureau or other agencies; allows you to see your file, to have incorrect information investigated, and to include your version of disputed items.

*Fair Credit Billing Act.* Establishes procedures for both consumer and creditors to follow if billing errors occur, or if there is a dispute over faulty items.

*Equal Credit Opportunity Act.* Prohibits credit discrimination based on sex, marital status, race, religion, age, or receipt of public assistance; requires creditors to give written reason for adverse action, and requires reporting to credit bureaus information in the names of both husband and wife if both are using accounts.

*Fair Debt Collection Practices Act.* Establishes procedures and restrictions regarding the collection of debts by collection agencies.

For more information regarding credit, see *Money Management —Managing Your Credit* and Lewin's *Financial Fitness for Newlyweds.* These are both listed in the recommended reading list.

When is the best time to save? At every age there are excuses for not saving. In the early years, you are just starting out, buying a home, raising a family. During the mid-years, you are paying off the mortgage and financing the children's education. Income is beginning to plateau. Retirement brings a fixed income, possible living changes, and higher medical costs. Since there is never a convenient time, the best time to save is NOW!

The purpose of savings and investments is to reach your short and long term goals and to become financially independent. Equally important is the psychological effect upon the marriage. Now is the time to choose a systematic plan for using your money to meet needs and wants, to share with others, and to invest for further security. In his book, *How to Succeed With Your Money* , George M. Bowman outlines an example of such a plan, the "10-70-20 Plan." It is based upon the concept that as stewards of our money we have a need and responsibility to share with others. We do this by paying taxes and out of gratitude for God's goodness, pledging a tithe. After taxes and tithing, Bowman says to pay yourself *first* 10% of your net income for savings and investments, live on 70%, and have no more than 20% in debts. He emphasizes that following such a plan can ensure financial health no matter what your income.

Successful investment involves an understanding of the dynamics of how your money works for you. The importance of safety, liquidity, and yield cannot be overlooked. All investments have degrees of risk. Know the risk involved and what you can emotionally and financially afford to risk. Liquidity, the ability to convert quickly to cash, preferably without penalty or loss, is a factor if you should need to tap resources for short term goals. During times of volatile interest rates, liquidity allows the movement of funds to options with better yields. The rate of return, or yield, determines how effectively your money will grow. The percentage of yield, compounding of interest, and length of time become major factors. Yield must be at or exceed the rate of inflation in order to preserve the value of future dollars. The importance of compounding and yield is apparent as you look at the rule of seventy-two which shows how long it will take to double your money. You divide the interest rate into seventy-two. For example, if you receive 6% it will take twelve years to double your money, and at 12% you double your money in six years. If you are interested in learning more about the effect of compounding on investments, you will find two books by Venita VanCaspel most helpful, *Money Dynamics of the 1980's* and *The Power of Money Dynamics*.

You are living in an exciting time of more savings and investment options than ever before. The young and small investor is as welcome to participate as the more seasoned. You can choose from money markets, certificates of deposit, mutual funds, treasury bills, government or municipal bonds, stocks, and IRA's to name a few. It is imperative to know the facts necessary for making good decisions. There is a wealth of information waiting for your perusal. The public library is an excellent and free resource. Schools and financial institutions conduct classes and seminars in personal finances. You may wish to consult a certified financial planner (CFP) to assist you. Do not be discouraged if the amount you can save is small at first. What is important is your joint commitment to a plan of action which can guarantee your financial security.

Be a smart shopper and reap the rewards of your purchasing power. Like budgeting, borrowing and saving, good spending is a learned skill. The use of good buying practices can assure greater value for the dollar spent, better quality products or services, and a deeper personal satisfaction. This is a list of good buying practices.

—*Follow a delayed action rule.* It allows you both time to discuss and evaluate clearly. It is the greatest prevention against impulse buying. This approach is essential for all major purchases.

—*Buy from a list.* This is particularly important when buying groceries or shopping at a variety store. It prevents impulse buying.

—*Buy during seasonal sales.* The importance of budgeting ahead to take advantage of the savings of sales is demonstrated here.

—*Do not sign anything unless you have read and understood.* This can prevent anything from minor irritation to major legal hassles.

—*Check and research items.* Resources such as *Consumer's Report* and *Changing Times* can provide valuable information on products, services, and consumer rights and interests.

—*Investigate retailer's reputation.* Checking with the Better Business Bureau and getting references can prevent fraud, inferior products or services.

—*Guarantees.* All warranties and guarantees should be in writing. They should clearly state length of time, coverage of both parts and labor, and maintenance agreement.

As in the fairy tale *Snow White,* you will sooner or later want your "Castle of dreams come true"—a home, a place to call your own. Where to live? Rent or buy? Old or new? The options are many—apartment or duplex, single dwelling, townhouse or condominium, city living or suburbs, a hobby farm or mobile home. Many factors, both financial and emotional, come into play. Job security, chance of transferring, savings, tax bracket, housing needs, and life style are just a few that will influence your choices. This major decision obviously needs time for research and evaluation.

Couples frequently make the mistake of rushing into home buying because they feel rent money is lost revenue. They fail to realize that there is more to consider in ownership than monthly payments. It is wise to carefully analyze the true cost of renting vs. buying.

Mortgage payments, interest, taxes, insurance and maintenance can strain a budget. You will need to know how much house you can afford. Before you actually look at home possibilities, contact a banker, credit union, or other lending institution to determine what you can safely assume. Then look at homes in that price range. For example, if you determine you can finance a $75,000 home, look only at property costing $75,000. This will prevent you from "falling in love" with and being tempted to buy something you truly cannot afford.

A good way to test if you are ready for this venture is to set aside for six months the difference between what you are now paying in rent and the cost of your new home. For example, if your rent is $400 and the cost of living in your new home, including mortgage, taxes, insurance, maintenance, and additional utilities will be $1,000, place the difference of $600 into a savings account. At the end of six months, you will have a better understanding of the adjustments you need to make and whether or not your plan is comfortable and feasible. You will also have accumulated $3,600.

Give yourself time to carefully look at all aspects of this major purchase. Better Business Bureau studies indicate that home owners list seven principal reasons for regretting the purchase of a home:

1. They initiated the purchase with insufficient funds.
2. The house turned out to be more expensive to maintain and operate than they expected.
3. The house proved to be poorly built.
4. The property decreased in value over the years.
5. The family income decreased, making the house a burden.
6. They did not examine the house carefully enough before buying.
7. They grew dissatisfied with the neighborhood.

Every financial plan should include provisions for protection against risk or loss. This is accomplished through various forms of insurance. Although costly, the degree of protection can mean the difference between well-being and financial disaster. How much insurance you will need depends upon the amount of risk you can afford to take. Again it is important that you become knowledgeable in order to carefully plan your insurance needs.

The basic insurance concerns are: health, life, disability, homeowners or renters, and automobile.

*Health Insurance.* With the high cost of medical care, it is essential to have adequate hospital, medical and major medical coverage. There are group plans, private companies, Blue Cross/Blue Shield, and Health Maintenance Organizations. Review your policy regularly and update it as your needs change. Be particularly aware of the coverage for pregnancy and the newborn. If you have any questions, contact your insurance carrier.

*Life Insurance.* The average consumer seems to know little about life insurance, is inhibited by the jargon, and consequently relies strictly upon the agent's presentation. As a result you are frequently sold a policy that is not your best protection. It is important that you understand the basics of life insurance, (which are really quite simple) and then choose the policy which best meets your needs. The purpose of life insurance is to provide maximum financial protection for surviving family members if you die prematurely. A young family will need maximum dollar protection for minimum cost. Annual renewable term insurance provides this type of protection. The books listed as further reading under *Money Management, Insurance and Home Buying* especially those by Walter S. Kenton, Jr., and Spielman, Zelman and Sharp, are excellent resources. In her two books, Venita VanCaspel also includes a good analysis of life insurance.

*Disability Insurance.* Although Social Security provides disability insurance, it may be insufficient to meet your needs if you were unable to work for a long time. Check your disability benefits at work or consider an individual policy.

*Homeowners Insurance.* This covers home, personal property, and liability. It is important to insure for at least 80% of the home's current replacement value. Update your policy regularly.

*Renters Insurance.* This covers personal property and liability in your rental unit.

*Automobile Insurance.* It is extremely important to be adequately insured in areas of liability.

Your decisions regarding insurance and the gathering of necessary information will be considerably lessened if you have an agent who is well-established, informed, trustworthy, and truly interested in your welfare. It may be as important to shop for an agent as to shop for insurance.

The effective management of money, the wise purchase or rental of a home(s), and discrete use of insurance is a life-long process. For a couple to engage in this process, requires a mutual commitment to research, planning and sound management. When these factors are effectively combined with a steady income resulting from a solid choice(s) of career(s), a couple can make effective use of the money they will earn during their years of employment. Of course, we must appreciate that our financial resources are gifts from God. Although it is proper to use them to enhance our own lives and prepare for a more secure future, we are to share our gifts with others. If our gifts are used in a selfish manner, we may become ensnared in the trap of selfishness, hedonism, and materialism. These problems will destroy individuals and a marriage more certainly than will poverty.

*CHAPTER 10*

# God's Gift of Sex

Couples blessed with a sacred view of life and marriage will enjoy and find fulfillment in their sexual union. They will appreciate the reason God created us male and female and provided us with the gift of genital sex. They will want to gain a deeper awareness of God's reason for doing so.

Genital sex is that drive which is deeply embedded within each of us and which prompts us to desire a physical union with a person of the opposite sex. However, God-believing people must go beyond the recognition of the simple fact that we instinctively desire a physical union with a person of the opposite sex. We are expected to use our intellect and reason to understand why God gifted us with genital sex, and then to use our wills to exercise the gift in the way God intended.

Those who believe in God believe that the gift of sex is intended to serve both love and life. God has both provided us with the gift of sex so that two people who have commited themselves to each other for life will have a privileged way to express their love for each other, to symbolize their commitment to unity, and to intensify the depth of their love relationship. Although our love is shown for a multitude of people in many ways, God has intended that two people, who have stood before His altar, His ordained minister and His people, and proclaimed their promise to love each other all the days of their life should have an absolutely unique way in which to express, symbolize and intensify their love.

Frequently, engaged couples will ask why the priest is concerned about pre-marital co-habitation and pre-marital sex. They sometimes sarcastically quip, "That's the trouble with a celibate priest; he gets his vicarious kicks by talking with us about our sex life." However, the priest realizes that an engaged couple who are co-habitating or having intercourse simply do not understand God's purpose for sex. The priest wants to help them appreciate all God has intended for the sex relationship. The problems with non-marital sex are many, but a key problem is best stated in terms of relationship. God intends that intercourse be a marriage act, a symbol of their faith and permanent commitment to loving each other. Non-marital sex pretends to be what it cannot be, and so it is intrinsically dishonest.

Besides serving as an expression of love, God intends that sex serve life by providing a husband and wife with the opportunity to cooperate in the act of bringing forth new life—to be co-creators. It is because procreation involves the cooperation of the husband, wife and God that this act should not be referred to as a reproductive act. It is not as though a couple is like a machine stamping out children. Instead, it involves a husband, a wife, and God in the awesome act of creating a new life which has an eternal destiny. Truly, sex is a holy act in which God is intimately involved. One can imagine that God is present in the physical union of a couple, so that He can enter into the act, breathing a soul into that new life—a soul which is to live forever. Truly, intercourse transcends the here and now and touches the eternal.

Spiritual persons see beyond the simple, narrow, and trivial view the secular world holds of sex. The secular world looks upon sex as a game to be enjoyed between two fun-loving playmates, but God intends sex to be a sacred act. One need only read the "Song of Songs" to understand that God has intended that great pleasure be gained from intercourse. In the "Song of Songs" the Jews conceived of God's relationship with His people as similar to the relationship between a bride and her husband.

Although fun and pleasure are proper uses of sex, they are not the only meanings. Once partners bypass the unitive and procreative meanings of sex and use it only for pleasure, it is not long before sex becomes only "for the hell of it." Along with recognizing the need to keep sight of the unitive (love) meaning of sex, couples also need to honor and respect their mutual fertility.

We generally spend a life-time learning to appreciate sex. Junior high school students often seem to laugh their way through any sex instruction. High school juniors and seniors become more serious discussing sex because they may be beginning to experience feelings of love for a person of the opposite sex. However, the engaged couple becomes increasingly more serious about sex as they begin to sense all God has intended. However, we need to realize that as for all of God's mysteries, its meaning for us continues to unfold.

When Alice and I celebrated our first anniversary, we looked back thanking God for the gift of sex, patting ourselves on the back during this first year of marriage, for coming to understand all there was to know about sex. However, now as we leave behind the first twenty-five years of marriage, we wonder what more God is going to teach us through His gift of sex. Beyond the general recognition that there is always more to learn, we can recognize that most of us move through a stage of innocence and naiveté to stages of shame, self-consciousness, embarrassment and guilt, to a final stage in which we embark upon an ongoing and continuing effort to grow in the virtues intended to help us truly appreciate sex.

*Innocence and Naiveté.* We are reminded of this first stage when we see children who are not terribly concerned if they are wearing all their clothes, if someone watches them splash around in the tub, or if someone watches them go potty. Instead, they appreciate having someone to splash on and someone to cheer for them when they successfully negotiate the potty. This naiveté was demonstrated by a ten- year-old who walked into the grocery store asking for a box of Tampax for his little brother. When the curious clerk wondered why he wanted Tampax for his little brother, he replied, "I read in a magazine that with Tampax you can go swimming, ride horseback and play tennis and my little brother can't do any of those things."

*Shame.* The next stage is punctuated with feelings of shame, embarrassment, self-consciousness and guilt. Although most adults will not recall much of the innocence and naiveté, we may remember the self-consciousness, embarrassment and guilt associated with the second stage. We need only recall the feelings associated with the first group shower. I was so proud that I had finally made it from parochial grade school to public high school. The sissy stuff of recess had been replaced with phy ed. However, I had no idea of the trauma waiting for me in the shower room. There I stood, just lathering up and tickled pink because I had finally made it. Now I was with the big guys. Unfortunately, I glanced around and suddenly realized that not all ninth grade boys were created equal. It was with deep embarrassment and self-consciousness that I glanced down thinking I would trade my new bicycle for a fig-leaf, even a very small one.

The girls, who were in the locker room across the gymnasium, glanced around noticing each other's breast development. One ninth grade girl who was not as endowed as her eighth grade sister came home crying to her mother, "I am the only girl in ninth grade wearing hand-me-up bras." The mother sympathetically replied, "I know just how you feel. I am the only mother in the neighborhood wearing hand-me-up bras." When a self-conscious sixth grade girl began wearing a training bra, she was unfortunately unaware that the straps would show through her white blouse. She was reduced to three hours of unceasing tears when the sixth grade boys began pulling at the straps and mercilessly teasing her.

If an engaged couple is to live out the theme of the "Song of Songs" and to reveal and surrender themselves to each other, it is important that they be able to resolve this sense of shame and embarrassment. Part of the resolution revolves around being able to think through and put aside some of the false ideas that have been learned through the years. Men need to set aside the idea that they are supposed to be sex gymnasts or studs. Some of this "junk" was learned in locker rooms or in other conversations with the guys. Men may recall feeling like fourteen-year-old self conscious John Jacob

Jingleheimmer Schmidt who stood in the locker room listening to the "big boys" discuss their sex exploits.

Although John Jacob was unaware of the meaning of all they discussed, he knew it had something to do with sex, and he knew he did not do the kinds of things they were talking about. He drew the unfortunate conclusion that a real man is a mean, tough, beer-drinking cotton picker who can "lay any broad around." Other than developing a distorted sense of masculinity, he made the mistake of believing the "big jocks" who disguise their self-consciousness and inadequacy with false bravado. If John Jacob does not develop a more authentic sense of masculinity and of the meaning of sex, the quality of his relationship with girls may not only be adversely affected in his high school years, but he may carry this attitude into marriage. Once married, some men recall these old tapes and remonstrate themselves thinking, "I am so inadequate and so out of it that I will never be able to satisfy my wife." This sense of inadequacy may contribute to the development of impotence—the inability to maintain an erection during intercourse.

As much as men need to learn about their immeasurable worth, women need to understand that their worth and value is not measured by the size of their breasts, the narrowness of their waist or the width of their hips. They are precious in God's sight, He loves them and they *are not* canisters of flesh whose function is to turn on males. Once, when I was trying to dissuade a group of high school girls from wearing haltless halters and bikinis, a boy shouted, "Don't tell them that." Thinking this would be an effective teaching experience, I asked the young man to explain why he wanted the girls to wear halters and bikinis. With an appropriate amount of embarrassment, he mumbled, "Because it turns us guys on." I think he and his friends gained some appreciation for the truth that turning on men is not the primary purpose for which God created women.

It is interesting that evidence of this shame, embarrassment, and guilt is found between various cultures and generations. Alice and I thought our children, who were liberally educated, would escape the self-consciousness we thought naturally flowed from a repressive approach to sex. By the age of ten or eleven, even three locks on the bedroom door and five on the bathroom door would not have given our daughter the privacy she demanded. Thinking it might have been different with our sons, we were surprised when they demonstrated the same self-consciousness.

As a family of campers, believing that the family that camps together deserves what they get, we saved shower money by having mother and daughter shower together and father and sons shower together. This was acceptable until the boys reached age eleven or twelve. Then, on one of our camping trips, I said, "Come on guys, it's time to go to shower." They only tittered and self-consciously exclaimed, "Dad's gay, Dad's gay! We aren't going to shower with a gay guy."

This self-consciousness about sex is an experience common to generations and cultural groups. In fact, the story of Adam and Eve, as it is told in Genesis, sounds very similar to that of any teenager who has stood in the shower room after phy ed class. Since we seem intent upon repeating the mistake of our first parents, it is helpful to recall that God placed them in a beautiful garden explaining that they would not have to work, that they would not suffer from sickness, and when it came time to join Him in heaven, they would be spared painful death and would simply be assumed into His kingdom. However, God integrated an important condition into the agreement. He said we could live in Paradise as long as we recognized that He had already decided upon a moral code. Because of the gift of free will, we could decide to do the right (His will) or to do simply as we pleased. It was not up to us to decide what was objectively right or wrong. God had reserved that perogative for Himself.

God left it to us to spend the rest of time discovering the laws of an entire physical universe. However, morality was too essential to let us discover those principles throughout the next thousands of years. Unfortunately, Adam and Eve succumbed to the temptation of the deceitful one who told them that God did not have the corner on the knowledge market. Succumbing to this appeal to their pride, Adam and Eve decided that they would not only decide what *they* wanted to do, but that *they* would also decide what was right and wrong. We see this mistake repeated by an entire society which seems to be saying, "God, you may say that abortion, contraception and euthanasia are wrong, but we say it is right for us and our vote carries as much weight as does yours. Therefore, we are not doing anything wrong because we say it is right."

After Adam and Eve conceded to their pride, they, like the teenager, looked down and became aware of their nudity. Because of their shame, they seemed to turn their back on God. Although they ran and tried to hide from God, He came and asked, "Who told you you were naked?" (Genesis 3:11). The similarity of these incidents suggests that the shame, embarrassment, self-consciousness and guilt frequently associated with sex and the genitals is a function of original sin. If this is true, it follows that if sex is to be a satisfying and enriching experience, we must be involved in an effort to overcome the effects of original sin.

The problem of original sin is confronted by Baptism and the other sacraments as well as by coming to know, understand, and follow God's plan. In fact, the best lesson we can learn is to *Follow the Instructions of the Manufacturer.* We are the most human and the most happy when we are freely obeying God. It is most important that we begin to grasp and to respond to God's love. It is because some imagine God as the *Great Spy in the Sky* that it is essential to avoid a scare approach to sex education. God is frequently portrayed as the "punitivarian" who goes about waiting for a chance to zap transgressors. Some may recall the kinds of stories that have been told in an effort to keep us in line.

For instance, during a 1956 college retreat, the retreat master told us of an unmarried couple he had known who were not open to the grace God would share with them to live chaste lives. He explained that one night they were out and once again had intercourse. He went on to explain that on the way home, their car was struck by a train and the young woman was killed instantly. A pin could be heard to drop in the auditorium as he concluded by saying that the young man now had to live with his conscience and wonder if he had sent his girlfriend to the eternal fires of Hell.

Although it is easy to criticize the fear approach and to plead for an approach based on love of God, self and others, persons must also be made aware of the dangers inherent in behavior that violates God's principles. It is a fact that intercourse, when married or unmarried, consciously desired or undesired, leads to pregnancy. It is a fact that promiscuity contributes to the spread of venereal disease and that health risks are inherent in the use of some contraceptives and the practice of abortion.

It is also true that the fear of accidents and traffic tickets has caused people to stick rather closely to the fifty-five mile per hour speed limit. It is a fact that the fear that strict enforcement of drunk driving laws will lead to arrest, incarceration and fines has caused people to modify their drinking habits. The fear of cancer and social disapproval has contributed to a decline in the percentage of people who smoke. It is an undeniable fact that when made aware of the facts, the fear of negative consequences affects significant segments of society. It is also true that many people truly desire to please God and to spend eternity with Him. Unfortunately, many have been denied an opportunity to be educated about God's plan and expectations. When many of us are made aware that non-marital sex is sinful and hampers our salvation, our behavior is frequently changed. Although the warning is scary, Paul's admonishment that fornicators, idolators, adulterers, homosexual perverts, sodomites, thieves, misers, drunkards, slanderers, or robbers will not inherit God's kingdom is a helpful motivator to many of us.

In preaching his gospel of love, Jesus was very clear about the consequence of rejecting that gospel. Yet education regarding risks to health and eternal salvation must be undergirded by the plea to follow the instructions of the manufacturer because He truly loves us. The commandments have been given to help us, and as we know from civil law, ignorance of the law does not protect us from the consequences of the law. God keeps His eyes on us because He loves us and not because He wants to catch us at something. Parents who recall standing by and watching their infant children sleep will have little difficulty appreciating that loving parents simply want to gaze at their children. Of course, as they get older, the parents may have to get up later on in the night if they want to watch their teenagers sleep.

I recall when our son, who aspired to be a basketball player, was finally confronted by the reality that a five-foot tall mother and a father who was only slightly taller did not provide him with the genetic heritage required to be a basketball player. By the time he was half way through high school, some of his friends were a head taller. Poor Tim was still waiting for his growth spurt. Although he spent a good bit of time sitting on the bench, Alice and I were convinced that he sat better than anyone else. We were like the proud parents watching the military parade. As their son's company marched by, the mother commented, "Look, Bill, our Tommy is the only one in step."

God's love is like that, He does not want to zap us. In fact, God has revealed precisely the opposite. The parable of the prodigal son teaches us about God's loving mercy to repentant sinners who ask for forgiveness, and the image of the Good Shepherd teaches us of God's pursuit of the sinner in order to bring him or her back in the fold. We may imagine that God may even cry when the disobedience of His children gets them into trouble, or when they need to be chastised. Of course, like a good parent, He wants to help us. When His offers are rejected, He waits until we will accept His loving hand. Like the good parent, there is nothing that pleases Him more than to be asked to help. We can imagine that He would drop everything to help us. On the other hand, He has also revealed the eternal consequences of rejecting Him and that He will not force us to accept His love and His ways.

The secular gospel proclaims that sex will become more satisfying if people free themselves from any sense of propriety, learn all the right buttons for titillation, and become aware of the appropriate gymnastic exercises. Contrary to the secular message, the Spirit teaches that our sex life will become more satisfying, if in responding to the love God has for us, we walk closely in the path of His Son and become people of virtue.

To have a Christian sex life, it is important to develop the virtues of modesty, purity of heart, and chastity. Recalling that the secularists maintain that the primary challenges in marriage revolve around money, communication and sex, the Christian couple realizes that chastity, rather than plain and simple sex, is a more appropriate challenge to be embraced by a loving couple.

When one hears people refer to sex as a "piece of such and such" or "getting a little," one knows of the need for the teaching of the Catholic church. Sex involves a total commitment of self and a total receiving of the other. You give and receive the entire person and not just a little or a bit. It taxes one's imagination to truly believe that the problem in these marriages is sex. Unfortunately, the spouses who talk in this manner generally expect a marriage counselor to change the other spouse.

Other couples may gasp an enthusiastic "Yes" when they are asked if they want a better sex life. Unfortunately, some of the enthusiasm wanes when it is explained that if they want a better sex life, they should strive to become saints. Their naiveté about the value of holiness is transparent when they ask, "What does religion, God and holiness have to do with a good sex life?" In fact, God has everything to do with satisfying sex. If couples are able to relate to God as pure Spirit, they will enhance their capacity to relate to the spirit of each other. For it is on the spiritual level that profound intimacy is discovered.

It is frequently disconcerting to the secularist to find that spouses with the most profound spiritual lives also report having profoundly rewarding sex lives. The secularist operates under the delusion that religious people are hung up about sex. However, they are simply like the wise owner of an automobile who has read the manufacturer's instruction booklet and who is using the automobile as it was intended to be used. If other people put water in the gas tank, gasoline in the radiator, and anti-freeze in the transmission, it will not be long before they will have a pile of junk on their hands.

During the course of retreats with married couples, I frequently say that, "The holier the spouse becomes, the more appealing he or she will be to the other and the more satisfying will their sex life become." Of course, this is assuming the good will of the other spouse and that the spouse is attracted by, rather than repelled by, sanctity.

After hearing this, several spouses have explained, "I would have thought you were nuts if I had heard you say that five years ago. However, now that each of us has been walking more closely with the Lord, I appreciate the blatant truth of what you are saying." One woman explained that when she was on her honeymoon, she could not see how God fit into the scene permeated with perfume and sexy negligee. Now that she was walking more closely with the

Lord, she saw how intimacy with Him promoted a deeper closeness between her and her husband. Again, a reading of “Song of Songs” should help her understand the pleasure God intends for those who are using sex properly.

*CHAPTER 11*

# Family Planning

Developing the virtue of modesty increases the possibility of developing an appreciation for God's gift of genital sex. Since modesty hinges upon a recognition of our bodies as temples of the Holy Spirit (Romans 8:5-11) the modest person, by refusing to permit him or herself to be treated as a canister of flesh, acknowledges the Spirit of the living God who is dwelling within everyone. Thus, modesty seems to warn against wearing haltless halters or other seductive clothing.

I felt very sorry for two sixteen-year-old girls who were lying on a beach in their very revealing bikinis. They thought the two boys next to them only had an aesthetic appreciation for the curve of their hips, and they were unaware that one of the men was commenting, "Look at Big Red over there. I can hardly wait until I get into town, find the first broad I can get my hands on and...(various euphemisms referring to intercourse)." Men and women are surprisingly unaware of what sex means to the other and how each is stimulated and responds.

When our son Mike was fifteen years old, I walked into the room where we had our TV set and noticed that he was much more alert than usual. When I glanced at the screen, I noticed a woman in very revealing undress. I said, "Mike, you may not watch that! She is a temple of the Holy Spirit. Even though she does not expect us to value her true worth, we may not contribute to the evil of her believing that she is only a canister of flesh."

With that I flicked off the TV exclaiming, "Mike, when it is so easy to be turned on, we have to turn it off." I began to walk out of the room and turned to say, "Mike, a real man walks away from that." I patted myself on the back and returned to the other room comforted that I had provided our impressionable son with a lasting lesson about the immeasurable worth of people and the dignity of sex. However a moment later my self-satisfaction was shattered when Mike shouted, "Dad, I turned it back on to see if I am man enough to turn it off."

In truth, the challenge to reverence persons and honor sex is with us throughout life. During an eighth grade sex education class our pastor asked if we knew how long the sex drive would last. We had already been surprised because he indicated that he, as a forty-five-year-old priest, experienced some of the same passions as we red-blooded thirteen and fourteen-year-olds. He explained that he had recently asked Mr. Proventeur, who was the sixty-year-old head usher in our church, how long the sex drive would last. Mr. Proventeur replied, "Well, Father, I suppose until about age sixty-five." At that point, a woman walked by and Mr. Proventeur glanced at her, turned to Father Swanson and said, "Father, let's make that seventy."

Throughout our life we are challenged to understand the proper use of sex. We can never sit back thinking we have it all together. A tragedy such as divorce or the death of a spouse may precipitate a decline in virtues that are essential to living a fulfilled life. For instance, the death of a spouse may prompt the surviving spouse to compromise values that have previously seemed effectively integrated into his or her life. This unfortunate phenomenon is especially evident in the lives of many who endure the tragedy of divorce. Many a spouse who had been committed to the marriage and was victimized by the other spouse becomes embittered by the "cruel hand dealt to him or her." He or she may succumb to the short sighted view that, "God created us to be happy; I have been made very unhappy; I cannot be expected to suffer more, and thus sex outside of marriage is permissible for me."

God created our body with a myriad of nerve endings which are sensitive to the tender caresses of a loving spouse. Rather than to be crippled by the view that breasts are only to sell after-shave lotion, cigarettes and automobiles, spouses should appreciate that breasts serve a more profound function. Not only may they provide nourishment for infant children, but they also add to the satisfaction of a couple's sex life.

As a gentle husband caresses the breasts of his wife, they each become prepared to surrender themselves totally to each other in the conjugal embrace. Think of the difficulty of the woman who had been taught that intercourse was the price she paid for marriage. Consider the woman confessing to Father Swanson, "On four occasions, I pretended I was asleep when my husband approached me for intercourse." Being the great man he was, Father Swanson offered her a beautiful five minute teaching regarding the meaning of intercourse, God's plan, and how God intended for her to enjoy this act. He suggested that, not necessarily for her penance, but to gain a different view of sex, she initiate intercourse on four occasions. She called Father Swanson at 8:00 the next morning exclaiming, "Father! I am halfway through my penance and I will finish the rest tonight."

1. *Purity of the Heart.* The need for the virtue of purity of the heart which supports chastity has been constantly acknowledged by Pope John Paul II. During the Wednesday audiences which he conducted from September, 1979 to May, 1980, he stressed the need for growth in the virtue of purity. On one occasion he commented, "Husbands are not to lust after their wives." The media mocked him suggesting that he was hung up on sex and that he ought to be shipped back to Poland before he ruined the lives of any other people. Unfortunately, many contemporary reporters fail to see a spiritual dimension to life. They did not recognize that the Holy Father was reminding spouses that marriage did not give them license to treat their spouses as objects. The Holy Father's comment

reminded me of a wife who tearfully exclaimed, "My husband only seems interested in my breasts. He forgets they are attached to me!"

The development of purity of heart involves putting on the mind of God. That is, to be able to think of people as God thinks of them. "Blessed are the pure in heart for they shall see God." Imagine what a difference it would make in marriage and engagement if couples valued and esteemed each other as God values and esteems each of us. What would it mean if they perceived each other as tabernacles—sacred vessels? One of the continual themes developed by John Paul II is that each person is a sacrament—that Jesus dwells within us.

One husband, who had not integrated the virtue of purity of heart into his life, complained that the problem in his marriage was the Catholic church and her hang-up about birth control. He explained that ten years earlier he had tried to have his wife sterilized. He lamented that their physician was Catholic and would not cooperate with the procedure. As he complained about how much he had suffered during the years of rhythm with the abstinence and concern about pregnancy, he failed to mention the number of affairs in which he had been involved. Then, he rather joyfully exclaimed, "Three months ago I finally got her fixed." He was relatively unmoved by my comment that she was not a cat one takes to a veterinarian to have spayed. Three months after he had her fixed, he left his wife for one of the women with whom he had been involved during the previous years.

It is difficult to believe that the problem in that marriage was the Catholic church, sex or birth control. It is more believable that the problem was a failure to love and to grow in the virtue of seeing others, including his spouse, as God sees them. His problem, among others, was that he refused to see her as a whole person, and he wanted her primarily for sex.

Another woman lamented that she finally consented to a tubal because her husband, who did not want to "scar his masculinity" with a vasectomy, complained that his concern about pregnancy dampened his enthusiasm about sex. Not only did he simply drop her off at the hospital for her surgery, but he left her a few months later for a more "swinging life." Time and again people misidentify the problem as being one of birth control when the authentic challenge revolves around truly understanding sex and accepting the challenge to be more totally loving people.

Since the development of purity of heart is aided by an appreciation of the way in which God loves His people, it helps to turn to Scripture to read about the love God has for His people. Psalm 139 is one of the many places in which we are provided a beautiful description of God's love. In this Psalm, we are told that God knows and examines us, that he knows what we are going to say before the word is even on our tongue, that He shields us, that He is wherever we are, that He created us and put us together in our mother's womb, that He watched us as we were being knitted in the womb of our mother, and that He listed and recorded our days even before the first of them occurred. Beginning to grasp the scope of God's love, David concludes:

> God, examine me and know my heart,
> probe me and know my thoughts;
> make sure I do not follow pernicious ways,
> and guide me in the way that is everlasting (Ps. 139:23-24).

2. *Chastity.* Chastity, as the umbrella virtue guiding the use of sex, includes and assumes modesty and purity of heart. Simply stated, chastity involves the proper use of sex according to our state in life. Thus, the celibate expresses chastity through perpetual virginity, and the engaged and other unmarried persons by a willingness to reserve intercourse for marriage. Spouses express chastity both by engaging in intercourse and by a willingness to delay intercourse.

Although the secular value frequently dictates that sex is one of the most common problems in marriage, a further examination of the statement reveals that individuals complain that there is not enough sex, too much sex, not the right kind of sex or that the gymnastics are not satisfactory. As this limited notion of sex floods the minds of couples, resistence to lust, sensuality and concupiscence is considerably reduced. Christian couples know that sex is a gift from God and that it is good. However, they also appreciate that sex is only a part of the whole of marriage. The single-mindedness of those whose primary emphasis is sex places them in the same position as the pilot who announced, "Good afternoon, ladies and gentlemen. This is your pilot speaking. We are flying at an altitude of 35,000 feet and a speed of 700 miles per hour. I have two pieces of news to report. One good and one bad. The bad news is that we are lost, but the good news is that we are making excellent time."

As sex is seen as an entity isolated from the whole of Christian marriage, couples fall prey to the sales techniques and influences of starkly materialistic groups such as Planned Parenthood who even invade maternity wards peddling their contraceptive wares. The alert Christian couple knows their spiritual sensitivities will be dulled if they are dominated by materialism.

3. *Chastity for the Celibate.* In exploring the gift of chastity, it is important to realize that chastity does not so much refer to having or not having intercourse, but more specifically to the proper use of God's gift of genital sex. Thus, for the celibate, chastity is expressed through a willingness not to marry, and consequently, not to engage in intercourse. In a sense, this expression of chastity testifies to the importance the Catholic church places upon marriage and the conjugal embrace. In preserving the gift of celibacy, the church is asking her vowed religious and ordained clergy to witness to the importance of God's Kingdom through celibacy.

4. *Chastity for the Married.* Marital chastity is concerned with the authentic expression of marital love through intercourse. A moment's thought reveals that not every act of marital sex is an authentic act of marital love. Marital rape is condemned by *Humanae Vitae,* and it is illegal in several states. Moreover, it is important to know that marital love is only partially expressed through intercourse; that is, intercourse is intended by God to be a unique expression of marital love, but only one of many. For every time a couple expresses love through intercourse, there will be many times in which their love is expressed by a willingness to delay intercourse. There are times couples delay intercourse as a way of honoring their fertility. That is, if it is the fertile time and a pregnancy would be inadvisable, the couple may delay intercourse so their love can be

shown to others, such as their children or parents. It seems that during the first several years of marriage, spouses spend a good bit of their time with a child in wet diapers sleeping between them.

If it is not that a child is sleeping between them, he/she may be disturbing them as did our son, Mike, when he was three years old. He entered our bedroom at a time when he was not the most welcome guest. As I voiced my displeasure, he walked over naively exclaiming, "Well, Mom and Dad, I just came to tell you how much I love you."

There are other times when intercourse is delayed because of what Alice and I frequently referred to as double jeopardy. That is, when the flu bug hits the household and one child is expelling from the front end and the other from the back. An incidence such as that has a very negative effect on one's desire for intercourse and intensifies the willingness to delay.

We were impressed with the meaning abstinence may have to children when our boys were sixteen and eighteen. Each of them had been terribly sick for several days. However, on the day of Mike's eighteenth birthday, they were each able to come to the table for a bit of ice cream and birthday cake. After we had sung "Happy birthday" and Mike had blown out the candles, he said, "I think we ought to have a great big cheer for Mom; she has been super these past days." It was reassuring to find that an eighteen-year-old could see that his mother had truly been giving of her total self to him and his brother. Although there had not been much of an opportunity for intercourse, a great deal of love had been shown.

We were struck with the importance of a willingness to delay intercourse when my mother, who was terminally ill with cancer, came to live with us. The whole family (and especially Alice) was kept very busy caring for her. As Alice again gave of her total self to my mother, I was able to see how the expression of our love was going way beyond our own conjugal relationship and being lived out through the care of my mother.

It is essential that we know the many ways in which love can be expressed. The Catholic church teaches that marital chastity excludes any use of unnatural forms of birth control including contraception, mutual masturbation, sodomy and sterilized intercourse. It teaches that contraceptive intercourse is not an act of love.

5. *Chastity for the Engaged.* It is because of the unique situation of the engaged that it is important to stress that love is sometimes expressed by a willingness to delay intercourse. The engaged are living in a highly erotic and permissive age which seems governed by a shoe-shop morality. This crude principle implies, " As much as you wouldn't buy a pair of shoes without trying them on first, neither should you marry someone without having sex with them."

This dehumanizing mentality overlooks several principles and truths. First of all, you simply do not experiment with carnal sex to determine the personal and deeply intimate compatibility you want in marriage. Sex is not intended to be the kind of gift which you try out with various persons and then choose the one with whom you experience the most satisfying sex. As much as, in general, the spouses are going to spend their marital life revealing themselves to each other, they are going to spend their marital life learning about sex. Rather than to enter marriage with the idea that they are absolutely compatible "in bed," it is more important to be committed to work lovingly at this dimension of their life. It should also be recognized that if experience counted, prostitutes and gigolos would make excellent marriage partners. In reality, these unfortunate, abused and violated persons make poor marriage and sex partners.

Some engaged couples protest that their love is so strong that the only way in which they can properly express it is through intercourse. They explain that unfortunately they are unable to marry at this particular time and yet it would be impractical to delay expressing their love through the powerful act of intercourse. These deceived but perhaps well-intentioned couples must be asked to explore the previously mentioned idea that deep, intimate and powerful love is frequently expressed (and sometimes *must* be expressed) by a willingness to delay intercourse. In this instance, their willingness to delay intercourse would be motivated by a desire to obey God's law. Although they will not totally understand the mind of God, it is possible to follow His plan even when the reasoning is not totally clear. Christ never said, "Understand me," but He did say, "Follow me," and that's what Christian discipleship is all about.

A brilliant, sensitive and extremely competent physican explained that his wife returned from Mass one day saying that she had prayed about a certain distance she felt was developing in their marriage. She said that she had the very clear impression that God had said, "Follow the teachings of my church in the area of birth control."

Her scientifically and technologically-oriented husband was less than impressed with the revelation she received. Yet, he loved and respected his wife, and he knew that she was not some sort of kook getting messages from the heavens. Thus, they veered from the use of contraceptives and returned to the practice of Natural Family Planning.

Some ten years later, he explained that he could never have imagined God would have so profoundly blessed their marriage. He explained that they had tapped a peace, warmth, and level of intimacy which was previously unfathomable. During these past several years, we have had the opportunity to meet with approximately 2,500 engaged couples a year. During these retreats with the engaged, we explain that because of the influence of the larger society, many couples may have been unaware of the real meaning of chastity. Now they have a desire to practice what can be referred to as secondary chastity—returning to a life in which sex is used properly. For some, this meant breaking up a co-habitating relationship.

We are privileged to run into some of these couples weeks, months, and sometimes years after a retreat. We have been impressed with the number of people who have said, "An awful lot happened to us during that retreat and one of the several decisions we made was to begin to abstain from intercourse until marriage. We were amazed at the way God blessed our relationship as we sought to bring our life more in line with His expectations."

The same comment is frequently heard in relation to Natural Family Planning. Couples explain that at first they were closed to the idea of Natural Family Planning and totally committed to the Pill. However, after some months of marriage, their life became so frustratingly chaotic that they decided to learn and to practice Natural

Family Planning. These couples explain that they are surprised by the intimacy which develops between them. Of course, this is not meant to imply that a life of chastity is not without frustration.

During the course of an engaged couples retreat, one unfortunate woman complained that we did not understand the dilemma of many of the women. She explained that she had to live with her fiancé. When asked to explain, she said, "Well, in case he needs it." When pressed further to find out what was meant by "it," she used a couple of more euphemisms and then said, "Well, you know, in case he needs to relieve himself."

When this twenty-five-year-old woman was asked if she was referring to intercourse, she rather reluctantly responded, "Yes." She went on to add that Natural Family Planning, because of the aspect of abstinence, would be totally impractical. She believed love demanded that she take the Pill so that she would be available in the event her husband needed to relieve himself.

This unfortunate woman telephoned me two years after this conversation explaining that they had not kissed each other in over two years and that they had not had intercourse in over eighteen months. She explained that on the previous afternoon she looked in her husband's billfold where she found a condom. As he was going out that evening she asked him, "Tom, what is the condom for?" He nonchalantly replied, "In case I find something." She was married to a man who had no understanding of the meaning of sex and no appreciation for the value of persons.

The Catholic church is one of the many churches that is concerned about an individual's freedom to marry as well as an individual's freedom not to marry. There is concern that pre-ceremonial sex and co-habitation compromise one's freedom not to marry. That is, a very good person who is interested in the virtuous life, may feel "I have shared myself on this most intimate level and now I must marry." It is important to understand that whether or not intercourse has occurred, whether or not a couple is co-habitating, and whether or not they are pregnant, they do not have to marry.

## How and Why?

Any discussion of chastity also involves a discussion of birth control. In approaching this delicate topic, it will be helpful to consider five recommendations.

1. *Study the Medical Side.* If an engaged couple is considering a means of conception control other than Natural Family Planning, study the available means of conception control. Since the contraceptive Pill is most frequently selected by younger people, special attention should be given to it. It is especially important for men to study the Pill. A man may want to go to a medical library or to the office of his physician and ask to read the *Physicans Desk Reference.* This reference includes a description of most medications. If you look for the contraceptive Pills, you will find a description of their composition, their indications, contraindications and side effects. One must question how a man who is knowledgeable about the Pill could bear to have his wife risk her health by using it. Furthermore, the Pill has abortifacient properties. That is, it may act as an early abortion agent. In considering this, it must be realized that fertility is a healthy and not a diseased condition. One is taking a drug to alter a normal condition rather than to correct a pathological condition.

Of course, it should be appreciated that the intrauterine device works primarily as an abortifacient and that the other mechanical and spermicidal means of conception control lack effectiveness and are aesthetically displeasing.

2. *Consider the Sociological Effect.* Secondly, along with study of the physiological side of birth control, examine the sociological effect. For instance, in the mid sixties when the Pill was accepted on a rather massive scale, it was thought that in freeing people from unwanted pregnancies not only would the population be reduced but marriages would be enriched. Although it is true that the birth rate has been reduced, it is difficult to justify saying that contemporary marriages are of a superior quality than those prior to the mid 60's.

3. *What About the Moral and Spiritual?* Also examine the spiritual and moral dimensions to the birth control question. It is now that one may begin to appreciate the chasm that exists between

various denominations and religions. Until 1930, all Christian denominations (and many other religions) agreed that unnatural methods of birth control were immoral. However, in 1930, the Anglican Lambeth Conference reversed its previous teaching by saying that unnatural methods were not always evil. Remember, they did not say they were good, they only said they were not always evil. It did not take long before various other denominations echoed the teaching of the Anglicans.

However, the Catholic church continued to teach that contraception was intrinsically dishonest. Although this can become very complicated, the essence of the Catholic teaching is that although one may choose to abstain from intercourse during the fertile time, it is not proper to directly attack the procreative dimension of sex. Whenever the gift of sex is exercised, there is to be an openness to both the affective and procreative meanings. During these times of loving abstinence, a committed couple may want to pray:

> Dear Jesus, we desire to share ourselves physically with each other, but through the strength of your grace we will contain that desire at this moment and wait until another day to enjoy the gift of the conjugal embrace given to us by your Father. For now, the warmth of your grace will enable us to feel united to each other through the words of love.

The next point in the teaching revolves around concern about means and ends. For instance, people question the difference between contraception and abstinence. They ask, "As long as the intention is to delay the pregnancy, does it make any difference whether the pregnancy is delayed through the use of contraception or by abstaining from intercourse?"

The Catholic church believes that it is necessary to use honorable means to achieve an honorable end. Although it may be honorable to delay conception, the Catholic church teaches that honorable means must be used to achieve that end. She believes that it is dishonorable to destroy the procreative meaning of sex in order to delay conception. This view is based upon the truth that fertility is an intrinsically good and healthy function. The Catholic church is concerned about the meaning of significant acts, and the marriage act is intended by God to be at least implicitly a renewal of the marriage covenant. Contraception contradicts this intrinsic meaning of marital intercourse and, is therefore, viewed as a lie. In marriage we commit ourselves to an unreserved pledge of faith, risk and caring love.

In an effort to gain a deeper understanding of the essence of the teachings that have been summarized, you may want to consult the recommended readings. It should be recognized that it is easy to find Catholics who disagree with the teaching of their church. Since it requires little effort to find dissenters from the teaching, the real challenge is to pray for the grace to begin to understand why the Church has continued, in spite of tremendous pressure to the contrary, to proclaim this teaching.

4. *Understand NFP.* Do yourself a favor of making a very thorough study of Natural Family Planning. In considering this recommendation, do not become hung-up on the old jokes and stories about rhythm such as, "What do you call people who practice rhythm?" "Parents!" Or "Gamblers—practicing Vatican Roulette." To compare the present knowledge about fertility with that of the 1930's is like comparing the contemporary practice of dentistry to that of the same era. Much more is known now than when Natural Family Planning was referred to as Rhythm.

Even when Alice and I were married, in 1959, the only sign we had of her fertility was that her temperature rose slightly after ovulation. Contemporary couples can come to an awareness of additional signs of fertility and also have access to some very fine instructional programs. A list of resources is included at the end of Chapter 12.

Although various approaches to Natural Family Planning place different emphasis upon the various signs, spouses should be aware that just prior to ovulation, a woman notices a very distinct mucus in the vaginal area. This is generally a sign that ovulation is about to occur. As a woman becomes more skilled in identifying the mucus, she becomes aware of the meaning of various textures. In fact, Natural Family Planning can be effectively practiced through an awareness of how the mucus signals fertility and infertility even when the other signs are ignored.

There are other NFP programs that emphasize the need to be aware of all of the signs of fertility and to use them for a cross-checking during the learning period. After a couple has gained experience they can stay with the cross-checking approach or choose a single-symptom approach. The cross-checking system is called the Sympto Thermal Method. Along with the mucus, a woman also can notice that ovulation affects her cervix. For instance, during the fertile time, the cervix becomes more open and soft like the lips. The presence of mucus usually corresponds with the open and soft cervix. A woman may also notice that at the time of ovulation she will experience a pain or discomfort in the area of one of her ovaries. This sign is not noticed by all women or in all cycles, but its presence is considered to be very close to ovulation. Then, subsequent to ovulation, a woman's basal body temperature elevates some .4 to .6 of one degree Fahrenheit.

The physiological key to Natural Family Planning revolves around the ability to determine the times of fertility and infertility. Modern Natural Family Planning even enables couples to determine the days of maximum fertility within the time of overall fertility, something very important for couples of low mutual fertility.

Couples who want to avoid pregnancy abstain from intercourse about three to six days prior to ovulation and for three to four days subsequent to ovulation. The purpose of the abstinence prior to ovulation is to allow for the death of the sperm. The reason for the delay after ovulation is to allow for the death of the egg.

This is only a brief description of Natural Family Planning which is essentially as effective and reliable as any other available means of conception control. But beyond the effectiveness of NFP, it is important to recognize that it is reversible, aesthetically pleasing, and the only form of birth regulation that is morally correct. However, it is essential to receive competent instruction and to be motivated to make effective use of this means of conception control. If the rules are not followed, Natural Family Planning will be about as effective as relying upon the Pill, yet occasionally forgetting to take it.

5. *What About Spontaneous Sex?* The final recommendation revolves around encouraging people not to become terribly hung up on the expectation of spontaneous sex. Whether or not I was a Catholic marriage counselor with a deeply internalized conviction about the truth of what we are teaching, I hope that I would have enough sense to alert people to the dangers of the expectation of spontaneous sex. This expectation generally is based upon the belief that the urge for sex is to be immediately satisfied. For instance, a newly married couple may stop off at a fast food place on their way home from work and order their favorite meal of a cheeseburger, fries and soft drink. However, they may order only one of each because they want to celebrate their oneness—and because it is near the end of the month and they are broke.

When they arrive home, they may sit down at their kitchen table, divide the food and begin to eat. Then, they begin hearing soft romantic music. As they munch their hamburger and fries (which is quickly washed down with a soft drink) they may be irresistibly lifted from their chairs and magnetically drawn towards each other. After another bite or two of hamburger and fries (washed down with a soft drink) they may gently and tenderly caress each other.

Then, they may look to the left and to the right and behold, they are enveloped by a cloud—purple for passion. After another bite of fries and a swallow of soft drink, they may embrace more passionately, grab another quick bite, wash it down, and then a breeze comes through the kitchen, picks up their purple cloud and carries them down the hallway to the bedroom. As their clothes are falling to the left and right, they may need to think of the day that they will have children and need to go back to pick up the evidence. Our son, Mike, came in to me one morning holding a piece of Alice's clothing and exclaiming, "Dad, it looks like you got a little frisky last night."

As the cloud descends over the bed and the breeze dissipates, the couple will fall helplessly and hopelessly into the marital embrace. All this would be pretty nice if it happened that way. However, the expectation of spontaneous sex frequently detracts from the potential of the conjugal embrace. This is simply because spouses often do not leave enough time for intercourse. This is only one of the many reasons Natural Family Planning can be beneficial to a couple. In talking about their desire (or lack of desire) for a pregnancy and discussing the signs of fertility, they need to plan whether or not they will have intercourse, and then allow for the time.

It seems that many couples practice one of the most effective forms of birth control there is—watching television or playing on a few different football, bowling or softball teams, or working a couple of jobs. In failing to allow sufficient time for intercourse, they may find themselves stumbling to bed along about midnight.

If they do not immediately fall asleep, the husband may be thinking, "I've got to be up at 5:00 in the morning and yet all the guys at work are talking about how often they have intercourse. It's been three days for us and she did have that book on homosexuality open again last night. Oh, well, I guess I'd better."

As he slaps his arm across the back of his wife, she may pray, "Dear God, if you really dwell among us, please help me now. I've got to be up at 6:00 in the morning and I am in no mood for sex. Yet is has been three days and he had that book on frigidity open again. Oh,well, I guess I'd better."

That often repeated scenario does not sound romantic. Natural Family Planning truly holds out much more for loving couples. It is because of my experience in marriage counseling that I am compelled to recommend Natural Family Planning. In so many instances, contraception either contributes directly to marital problems or it denies couples the opportunities to build the kind of character and virtue that will help them resolve or avert problems.

As a result of our contact in retreats for married couples, we are aware of the way in which Natural Family Planning can enrich marriages and of the way in which artificial contraception contributes to chaos and denies spouses the opportunity to grow in character and virtue. Of course, very especially, we are aware of what Natural Family Planning has meant to our own marriage.

Although I feel sad when anyone resorts to contraception, sterilization or abortion, I feel even more regret when this is resorted to by the newly married. It was only after several years of marriage that we had the opportunity to attend the NFP classes offered by the Couple to Couple League. They were so beneficial to us and have been so beneficial to thousands of other couples that newly married couples will not want to miss what NFP can bring to their marriage. Most certainly, NFP is not *the* easy answer to birth control. Of course, *the* answer has not yet been found. Neither is it *the* answer to love. But NFP is more effective than most available means of conception control and about as effective as any means short of total abstinence or removal of the ovaries or testes. Because of the way in which contraception can feed selfishness, it can threaten a couple's love relationship. On the other hand, the tenderness, awareness and consideration needed to effectively practice NFP can promote a couple's love relationship and help them learn to be magnificent lovers.

Contraception makes it too easy to slip into the trap of selfishness, and it grossly interferes with the effort to become loving people. After all, in accepting the call to be spouses, we are challenged to become intense lovers. Although Natural Family Planning is not the be-all and end-all of marriage, it is one of the many ways in which we learn to be magnificent lovers.

# CHAPTER 12

# The Honeymoon

A mental attitude towards intercourse and a commitment to living a life of virtue are more important than the physiological dimension of sex. In this same way, a constellation of physiological, emotional and psychological factors operate at the time of the honeymoon. A honeymoon provides an opportunity to adjust to new feelings toward each other and to recuperate from the tension and excitement of the wedding.

If a couple truly believes the wedding is a time to visit the home of their Father, ask for His blessing, and ask our Lord and Savior to join them as three-in-one, they will feel the effects of supernatural grace. This will cause them to feel differently toward each other. Perhaps the song "He Touched Me" best expresses what can happen. The couple will realize that Jesus unites them in a way they had not imagined possible. The honeymoon provides an opportunity to adjust to this deeper more intense union.

Couples have different ideas about the way to celebrate a honeymoon. Because of the multitude of preferences possible, only a few definite do's and don'ts will be suggested. Most likely, a couple will be very busy during the weeks before the wedding. To marry on a Friday night and leave on a midnight flight for a honeymoon in some distant exotic place is unwise. It is better to rest before taking off for the far reaches of the earth—or even the county. Since a honeymoon should be a time to rest and unwind, it is difficult to understand why a couple would drive 3,000 miles in seven days.

It is unfortunate, if instead of allowing time for a honeymoon, a couple insists on returning to work the next morning. Even more unfortunate is the couple who skipped a honeymoon because their wedding was the Friday night of the same weekend that the groom played in a softball tournament. A wedding should be more than just a break from the normal routine and should be more important than missing a few innings of softball.

Other than avoiding a honeymoon that will be fatiguing, it is advisable to avoid honeymoon resorts which advertise wall-to-wall or heart-shaped beds, sunken baths and the glory that was once Rome. Some honeymoon resorts place excessive emphasis upon the erotic, suggesting that the honeymooners will be surrounded by sand, sea, surf, and sex. This can only set up a couple for a frustrating and disappointing experience. When a couple celebrates their Silver Wedding Anniversary, they may enjoy the comfort of such a resort without false expectations of exotic romance.

It is advisable to plan an affordable and relaxing honeymoon which does not place excessive emphasis upon the erotic. During a weekend retreat with engaged couples, Alice and I had lunch with three couples who discussed their honeymoon plans. One couple proudly explained they were taking a Caribbean cruise and another said they were going to a nearby metropolitan area. The third couple remained silent mumbling, "We're going to West Fargo." That was a city just a few miles from where they were being married. After the others left, Alice commented, "I wish you wouldn't be so self-conscious about going to West Fargo. You're doing something you can afford; you won't have a lot of travel, and you will be in familiar surroundings. Anyway, West Fargo is probably a pretty good place." It's quite probable that their honeymoon did include these suggested advantages. It may be surprising to learn that a number of couples plan a camping trip for their honeymoon. As long as it is something to which they are accustomed and mutually enjoy, it may be a good idea.

It is wise to avoid Uncle Ole's advice. Frequently, a couple has an "Uncle Ole" who has been unhappily married for years and who insists upon giving everyone his formula for an unhappy marriage. Uncle Ole usually explains to his niece, "Well, Mavis, you're going to be finding yourself in a hotel room with that red-blooded boy and you will have to be relaxed." He then suggests that Mavis have a couple of drinks. Quite possibly, Mavis is not accustomed to drinking—especially on her wedding day. A couple of drinks may be just enough to get her barfing all over the place—not too romantic!

Rather than listen to Uncle Ole, it would be better to demonstrate the ultimate consideration toward each other. On their honeymoon the couple will experience the effect of having made a total and life-long commitment to each other. Brides often comment that they appreciated that their husband left the room for five or ten minutes, providing them with a few minutes alone. Beyond this, there is no eleventh commandment stating, "Thou must have intercourse the first day of marriage." In fact, some couples agree not to have intercourse on the first day of their marriage. For some this agreement is prompted by a recognition that the stresses of the day may not be the most conducive to a positive experience. There are others who do this as a way of demonstrating that they married for far more than sex. Several brides have confided that, when they began intercourse, their husband, sensing their tenseness or fatigue, lovingly suggested, "We need not have intercourse tonight; we've got tomorrow and, really, the rest of our lives."

Of course, if after a month, one or the other is still too tense or fatigued for intercourse, they have a problem to which it would be advisable to pay attention. It is surprising to meet with couples who have been married for over a year and have not yet had intercourse. Since very competent help is available to help couples with these problems, it is wise to attend to them before hurt, fear and anger create an almost irretrievable breakdown. This applies to all areas of marriage and not only the sex relationship.

Those dedicated and committed couples who have practiced premarital chastity, are planning to use Natural Family Planning, and who do not believe they should achieve pregnancy during the first several months of their marriage may feel cheated if they are in phase II (the probably fertile phase). Although we occasionally need to be reminded that we should not marry until we are able to lovingly receive children into our lives, it is understandable that conscientious couples may want to delay a year before pregnancy. If this is the case, it can only be suggested that couples who have a deep love for God, for His plan and for each other would need to abstain from intercourse during all or part of their honeymoon. They could also decide to delay their honeymoon for a few days.

Although a bride and groom may not be enthralled about the reminder that abstinence can be a powerful way of showing love, their consternation may be mitigated by the realization that some couples have observed a tradition of abstaining from intercourse on their wedding night. The couple who will lovingly practice NFP will be faced with many times in which the time of coital rest may be inconvenient. In physically expressing their love during the time of abstinence, a couple is faced with the question they faced during the time of their courtship. That is, "How far can we go?" The answer remains much the same as it was during the courtship. That is, if intercourse is not intended, spouses should temper their caresses in such a way that they do not become aroused to the point that one or both of them reaches a climax.

It is unfortunate that couples sometimes refer to the time of coital rest as a time during which they cannot show their love, make love or be loving towards each other. These expressions fall short of reality. During the time of coital rest, spouses show a profound love and respect for God, their church, the other, themselves, for the children they already have, for the children they may have in the future, and for the integrity of intercourse. They are merely saying that they will not use the gift of intercourse as a way in which to express their love. It is essential that these dedicated spouses continue to love each other in such a way that this time of abstinence does not become interpreted as rejection of each other.

Most of us need tender physical contact and reassuring verbal interaction which transmits a feeling of being loved and cared for. Loving spouses must be alert to the danger of appearing aloof, cold and rejecting when true love expects them to express their love and commitment in ways other than through the conjugal embrace. In learning the art of controlled caressing, spouses become aware of the variety of ways in which they say, "I love you." When spouses know they are loved and cared for, it may be less difficult to delay intercourse. During this time of coital rest, it is important for spouses to remain close to each other and to reassure and be reassured of their love. Spouses will be helped in their ability to experience and express love if they concentrate on being simple, tender, gentle, and understanding persons.

One spouse, who misunderstood the virtue of chastity, asked how they could go from being very sexually active to being periodically and routinely chaste. Growth in chastity contributes to the development of a meaningful sex life and involves both loving intercourse and loving abstinence. In some respects, it is possible to make too big a deal of abstinence. One of the most frequent questions asked by those being introduced to NFP is, "What do we do during the times of abstinence?" The answer should be as simple as saying that other than not having intercourse, they do what they usually do.

It is unfortunate that abstinence is sometimes looked upon as a burden. The attitude of some couples towards the time of coital rest, may be likened to that of *Mad Bart and Barbara* who resent the abstinence associated with NFP. They may have accepted this approach to birth control as a biologically and medically sound method or because their church has told them that this is the only morally acceptable means of conception control. Since they fail to see the positive features, the days of abstinence are filled with tension. During this time, they do little more than growl at each other, complain about the church and curse fertility.

*Frantic Fran and Francis* believe that intercourse is a powerful drive which may almost be necessary for physical and emotional survival. Thus, during the days of abstinence, they live by sublimation. They try to avoid each other, work hard, take plenty of cold showers, and do whatever else they can to drain off libidinal energy. They may find that softball, bowling or bicycling are effective ways to sublimate this energy.

The *Eager Beavers—Bea and Ben*— see the positive value of abstinence, believing they will realize more satisfaction from the conjugal embrace if intercourse does not become a dull routine. They believe abstinence helps them develop a more exciting conjugal relationship. However, they fix on the dynamics of the conjugal embrace and fail to see the total way in which abstinence can positively affect their marital relationship. They may clean house, wax floors and cars, bake bread and get as far ahead of their work as possible so that they can take maximum advantage of days on which they permit themselves to have intercourse.

*Normal Norma and Norman* believe that the complete individual has an integrated sense of the importance of working, playing and praying. They see abstinence as an integral part of their relationship, recognizing that it helps them develop a total appreciation for each other. Women seem to react with a feeling of warmth, happiness and desire toward a husband who respects her fertile phase—all the more desirous of future coital union. During these times of coital rest, a man can discover that he thoroughly enjoys the feeling of simply holding his spouse or being held by his spouse. When other avenues of expression are explored, mutual understanding will grow and intercourse will become a privileged way of expression, not the only way. The mature couple finds various ways to convey tenderness, affection, solace and understanding. Of course, it is very important that spouses be open to each other regarding their own feelings and sensations.

If NFP is to provide a means for achieving personal maturity and enriching marriages, it is important to grow in spiritual oneness. Those who yearn to be in close union with God are able to experience a deep sense of intimacy with or without intercourse. Rather than to think of keeping their distance during the time they choose to abstain from intercourse, spouses should realize that the spiritual intimacy, growing from a mutual union with God, will sustain them as they wait to express the oneness resulting in intercourse. It is helpful to remind ourselves of the depth of God's love. St. John reminds us, "Love, then consists in this: not that we have loved God, but that he has loved us and has sent his Son as an offering for us (John 1:4)." Or further on we read, "God is love and he who abides in love abides in God and God in him."

Many readers will recall the old story about the couple being advised that the secret to conception control during the fertile time was to pray the Rosary. When asked whether it should be prayed before or after intercourse, they were told, "Instead of." The advice deserves more than a snickering response. If Christ is not the center of our marriage, it is about as fair to say NFP is not working as it would be to make that claim when a pregnancy resulted from intercourse the day before ovulation.

A commitment to controlled caressing during the fertile time involves a recognition that caressing of the primary erogenous zones would more than likely arouse an irresistible desire for intercourse or cause the spouses to climax without having intercourse. If they have intercourse during the fertile time, they will probably become very anxious about pregnancy. The incidence of spontaneous intercourse coupled with the concern about pregnancy may precipitate an overall anxiety about sex and intercourse. Of course, if a pregnancy occurs, it is quite likely that NFP will be viewed as the culprit. If climax occurs, aside from intercourse, the integrity of sex and God's plan is compromised and the spouses may develop some habits that will contribute to the development of premature ejaculation, or a preference for self-satisfaction rather than the mutuality of intercourse.

It is important for couples to avoid the temptation to get into the "how-far-can-we-go-before-climaxing" game. This interaction involves relatively passionate love-making in which the spouses become very excited and aroused and seem to hope that a climax will not occur. However, the other side of this coin is that many couples explain that one of the things they like about NFP is that it provides them with the opportunity to enjoy the kind of love play they enjoyed prior to marriage, when because of their commitment to the proper use of sex, they had decided to save intercourse for marriage. However, they derived enjoyment from hugging, kissing, holding and caressing. Once they entered marriage, they found that they became a little careless about the love play and progressed more rapidly to intercourse than they may have liked. Some couples look forward to the times of coital rest when they know they will not have intercourse, but tenderly and gently caress each other. However, couples of this view need to be especially careful of the "how-far-can-we-go" trap.

Couples who are either learning or actually implementing the art of gentle caressing should remember that during the times of coital rest, "things go better with Pepsi." Many a couple finds that after a cocktail or two they believe they can support the world. Some couples, with a proclivity for martinis, have been tempted to nickname one or two of their children Olive. Normal Norma and Norman strive to develop a non-frustrating, slower pace of touch and physical closeness appropriate to the fertile phase of the cycle. They seem to remember that:

> Love is patient and kind;
> Love is not jealous, or conceited, or proud;
> Love is not ill-mannered, or selfish, or irritable;
> Love does not keep a record of wrongs;
> Love is not happy with evil, but is happy
> with the truth.
> Love never gives up; its faith, hope and
> patience never fail (1 Cor. 12: 4-7).

The tenderness and consideration associated with the honeymoon can only be a reminder of the qualities needed throughout the marriage. This works reciprocally—the characteristics necessary for a meaningful sex relationship are the same ones needed for creating a rewarding marriage.

For some years I was concerned that men were prepared for intercourse before their wives. This involved me in an ongoing argument with God in which I explained, "That's what happens when you aren't unionized. You worked a six-day week and then you came to our sex responses, you were tired and goofed!" God, tiring of this harangue, exclaimed, "Jack, be quiet! Won't you understand that if I created you with exactly the same pattern of response as your wife, you would have learned nothing from or about each other. What is learned during the conjugal embrace helps you during the other hours of your marriage. Similarly, what helps you in the rest of your marriage, helps you symbolize the union in your sex relationship, which I share with my Son and our Spirit."

During foreplay, the spouses prepare each other for intercourse by stimulating the erogenous zones. The thighs, vaginal area, clitoris and breasts are the primary erogenous zones for the woman. Essentially her entire body is an erogenous zone which is very responsive to touch. The penis is the primary erogenous zone for the man. As they learn more about each other, the partners discover ways in which caressing prepares them for intercourse. It will be helpful if the newly married partners recognize the importance of tenderness and patience, realizing they have a lifetime to learn this intimate language of love. It is a mutual learning process which requires that they help each other understand ways in which the conjugal embrace can be even more meaningful and pleasurable. They should not be surprised if they experience some discomfort or pain during their initial experience with passionate petting and with intercourse. Neither should they be unduly shocked and alarmed if their initial experiences are a bit emotionally uncomfortable or if they do not find it "all that much fun." Some newlyweds wonder why such a big deal was made out of sex. Again, distinguish between the serious problem which may telegraph the need for specialized help and the less traumatic situations in which "We need to grow together."

Although it is possible that Uncle Ole entered marriage very ignorant about sex and, not knowing what to expect, the risk for contemporary couples is that they may expect too much. Realistic expectations, consideration for each other, and a commitment to learning over time can combine to help a couple experience the union and ecstasy intended by our Creator. Needless to say, these traits should guide the couple from their honeymoon until the day they join God in heaven.

There is a risk that the sexual relationship may become a dull routine. It is vitally important that couples not fall into the ennui referred to earlier. After a couple months of marriage, a woman may be in the bathroom setting her hair in curlers and looking like she came through a cyclone. As she walks out in flannel pajamas and wool socks (if the temperature is below zero), she may present quite a challenge to Cupid. One husband lamented that he gave his wife a frilly nightgown for their honeymoon and did not see it again until their five-year-old wore it on Halloween. A husband may just have changed oil in the car and come into the house in a very romantic mood. However, he will look more romantic if he showers before he acts upon his notions.

When both the husband and wife are prepared for intercourse, the husband will begin penetration. A couple should not panic if they do not initially experience mutual and/or simultaneous orgasm. For some couples it may take several months before orgasm is mutually experienced. In fact, it is not unusual to talk with couples for whom it has taken some years before they have established that degree of understanding and compatibility.

Some brides may experience a condition identified as honeymoon cystitis. This is a mild vaginal infection caused by the irritation of the penis against the vagina. This is mentioned only to alert couples to the fact that a physician can effectively treat this condition with antibiotics.

Couples frequently express concern about how long intercourse is to last. Answers to such questions must be individualized. Ultimately, the answer depends upon what mutually satisfies the couple. Perhaps our desire to be the "better than the average bear" prompts us to also be concerned about the frequency of intercourse. Again, this depends more upon the desires of a particular couple than upon national surveys. Couples will find that intercourse may be relatively infrequent if they are busy or preoccupied with some particular project. However, if they are on vacation or feeling especially relaxed, intercourse may occur several times in one day.

Couples should also recognize the importance of the immediate time after intercourse. This moment provides an opportunity to shut out the rest of the world and rest peacefully in each other's arms. They should also say something to the other about the meaningfulness of the experience. A little "thank you" is very helpful.

Our Father has attached immense pleasure to the marital embrace. The satisfaction derived from the sense of union that is achieved—a unity and oneness symbolizing the union of Father, Son and Spirit. As they give themselves as total gifts to each other, the coital embrace symbolizes the couple's surrender to each other. The couple begins to make the adjustments to marriage during the intense time of the honeymoon.

* * * * *

Most Family Life Offices of Catholic dioceses will have information about National Family Planning and about where instruction is given.

Other organizations from which information can be obtained regarding the availability of instruction in Natural Family Planning:

The Couple to Couple League
P.O. Box 111184
Cincinnati, Ohio 45211
(513) 471-2000

This organization has teaching couples throughout most of the United States and in some overseas countries.

Diocesan Development Program for Natural Family Planning
Seton Hall University
South Orange, New Jersey 07079
201-761-9647

An agency of the National Conference of Catholic Bishops which assists the various dioceses in their efforts to develop Natural Family Planning programs.

The Human Life Center
University of Steubenville
Franciscan Way
Steubenville, Ohio 43952
614-282-9935

Natural Family Planning Education of Rochester, New York, Inc.
Kearney Building
89 Genesse Street
Rochester, New York 14611

Serena Ontario
55 Avenue Parkdale
Ottawa, On. Canada K1Y 1E5
306-665-2522

An organization providing information about and instruction in Natural Family Planning.

Natural Family Planning Center of Washington, D.C., Inc.
Dr. Hanna Klaus
8514 Bradmoor Drive
Bethesda, MD 20817
301-530-9383

A U.S. referral source for the Ovulation Method.

Twin Cities Natural Family Planning Center
HealthEast St. Joseph's Hospital
69 West Exchange Street
St. Paul, MN 55102
(612) 232-3088

*CHAPTER 13*

# The Power to Love

As a high school girl gazes proudly at her boyfriend's class ring hanging from a chain around her neck, she remembers the times they have told each other of their love. As a woman looks affectionately and appreciatively at her engagement ring, she is reminded of the love she and her fiancé have professed for each other. As a man who is a thousand miles from home looks at his wedding ring, he is reminded of the life of love being lived by him and his wife. If it is true that a symbol or tangible piece of evidence of the love of someone dear to us comforts, reassures and warms our hearts, we should always be reminded of the love of our Father in Heaven.

If a ring, a bouquet of flowers, or a specially prepared gourmet meal serves as a sign of love, think of how powerfully we are reminded of God's love. Although a young man, smitten with an almost lethal dose of romantic love, may proclaim, "I will lay the entire world at your feet," God has in fact done this. In the first chapter of Genesis, we are reminded that whenever we look at a sunset, a sunrise, the moon, stars in the sky, the water in our oceans, lakes and rivers, the birds of the air, the animals, or a girl friend or boy friend, fiancé or fiancée, and spouse we are seeing evidence of God's love. He has, indeed, laid the world at our feet. All that is good is a gift from God and witnesses to His love for us.

When we look at all God has given us, we also become aware of the overwhelming diversity, scope and breadth of God's creative power. It exhausts our imagination to realize that nothing God has created is like anything or anyone else. Each snowflake, each flower of the same species, and each person is like none other. A girl friend or boy friend, fiancé, fiancée, or spouse is like no one else. No other person has the same voice, the same set of fingerprints, the same eyes. Everything about each of us is unique and to be treasured.

Yet, this fact of difference testifies to more than the diversity of God's creative power and to our uniqueness. It also testifies to the fact that our uniqueness is not a mandate to create our own law. Each person's uniqueness is to be used to build the community—the Mystical Body of Christ. Each of us is important and each has a unique contribution to make. The importance of this uniqueness is seen in the microcosmic community of the domestic church created by a husband and wife and their children. We each have unique contributions to make to the building of the relationship of love and to the development of the oneness and unity Christ envisions for all humankind and which existed in Paradise before Adam and Eve decided to disobey.

## Many Ways of Loving

Genesis reminds us that we are social beings who are not self-sufficient—we need other human beings with whom to share our lives. In building our lives together as husband and wife, we begin to see something of what our Lord means when he tells of "man and woman becoming two in one flesh." Two in one, is a hunger for oneness and it is this hunger that is the "stuff" of life. Love is not a question of *having, but of being.* When we learn to love poetry, it becomes part of us. We are more than we were before. When we learn to love our spouse, that love becomes a part of us. We are more.

However, God has not only given us the world and all that is in it, as a sign of His love, but, as the author and source of love, He has also given us the power to love. The loving apostle, John, reminds us:

> Beloved, let us love one another because love is of God; everyone who loves is begotten of God and has knowledge of God. The man without love has known nothing of God, for God is love. God's love was revealed in our midst in this way: he sent his only Son to the world that we might have life through him. Love, then, consists in this: not that we have loved God, but that he has loved us and has sent his Son as an offering for our sins. Beloved, if God has loved us so, we must have the same love for one another. No one has ever seen God. Yet if we love one another God dwells in us, and his love is brought to perfection in us. The way we know we remain in him and he in us is that he has given us of his Spirit. We have seen for ourselves, and can testify, that the Father has sent the Son as Savior of the world. When anyone acknowledges that Jesus is the Son of God, God dwells in him and he in God. We have come to know and to believe in the love of God for us. God is love, and he who abides in love abides in God, and God in him. Our love is brought to perfection in this, that we should have confidence on the day of judgment; for our relation to this world is just like his. Love has no room for fear; rather, perfect love casts out all fear. And since fear has to do with punishment, love is not yet perfect in one who is afraid. We, for our part, love because he first loved us. If anyone says, "My love is fixed on God," yet hates his brother, he is a liar. One who has no love for the brother he has seen cannot love the God he has not seen. The commandment we have from him is this: whoever loves God must also love his brother (1 John 4:7-21).

Since God is the author and source of love, we must be plugged into God in order to be empowered to love. A marriage or engagement, without God, is like trying to toast a piece of bread. We sometimes drop a piece of bread into the toaster only to realize, some ten minutes later, that the toast has never popped. Nine times out of ten, we find the problem was very simple—the toaster was not plugged in.

It is unfortunate that spouses and engaged couples are among those who sometimes treat religion as a nicey-nice thing that is more like icing on the cake. Religion and God are the very essence of marriage as they are of all life. If we accept that the primary challenge and purpose of marriage is to become Christ-like lovers who surrender ourselves to the welfare of another, we are beginning to be empowered to love. A marriage or engagement without God, is like trying to drive a car with one flat tire. Thus, people who desire to become great and magnificent lovers need to be willing to be plugged into God, who, as the author and source of love empowers them to love. William and Nancy Luellen explain that couples who are married in church and who continue to regularly attend church have a divorce rate of only one in fifty (2%).[11] And among couples who marry in a church, continue to attend church, and also have a prayer life at home, only one in 1,105 of these ( .09%) couples divorce. These figures taken from the 1980 census, illustrate the slogan, "The family that prays together stays together."

As one of His magnanimous acts of love, God created the human being in His own image and likeness. In the second account of creation, we read that God first created the male. This has prompted some to quip that, He realized His mistake and so created the female. Others have said that you always begin with the rough draft. Of course, to counter this, others have guessed that Eve was so named because she signified the end of Adam's perfect day. Genesis tells us that, by himself, Adam was lonely. We read that while man was sleeping, God took one of his ribs and built it into a woman. Upon seeing the woman created by our loving God, Adam exclaimed:

> This at last is bone from my bones,
> and flesh from my flesh!
> This is to be called woman,
> for this was taken from man (Gen. 2:23).

In lovingly giving us our sexuality and making man for woman and making woman for man, God expects us to transcend the obvious fact that each of us intuitively and instinctively desires a physical union with a person of the opposite sex. In transcending the basic goodness of this desire, we are expected to place it in the service of love and life. That is, when we use sex well, we are to use it to serve love and to serve life.

We traverse through various stages in a continuing effort to learn to be loving people. If we think of three-year-old Jonathan's love for Maria, we may wonder if he truly loves her or wants the cookie she has in her hand or to ride her trike or use her wagon. Then, does thirteen-year-old Jennifer really love Mitchell, or does her proclamation of her love help her feel good and grownup? What about the love between sixteen-year-old Mike and Barbara? Are the sages correct when they try to tell them they're too young, too young to really be in love? Mike and Barbara need to be aware that the sheer power of the sex drive, combined with the multitude of insecurities associated with entering young adulthood, can create confusion between the lust which seeks its own satisfaction and authentic love. Genuine love desires that which is good for the other and which is committed to serving the other. Although it sounds less romantic, Mike and Barbara might more honestly admit that they lust after, rather than love each other.

But somewhere along the way a special relationship develops to the point that each of the partners begins to say, "I think I am coming to the point of being as concerned about the welfare of this person as I am about my own welfare." To be as concerned about the welfare of the other as we are about our own welfare is a basic and elementary step in loving. As two people become increasingly convinced that they are becoming sufficiently mature to love authentically and that they are compatible, they may announce their intention to marry. Engagement announces an *intention* and not a *promise* to marry.

Through solemnization, couples invite Jesus into their lives. They pray that He will begin that process of preparing them for the oneness of marriage by melting into one their individual hearts by the flaming inferno of love bursting forth from His most Sacred Heart. The solemnization is a prayer for the grace to love as Christ loves and to live an engagement as He would wish. It is to want that which is best for each other and consistent with Christ's will.

Engagement witnesses to a couple's belief that their relationship has matured to the point that they have transcended the selfishness and narcissism of the adolescent years and that, now, they are able to go beyond the "I" and the "me" and to think in terms of "we" and "us." Although they appreciate the importance of their individuality and that what each of them thinks, wants and feels is important, they are also aware of the value of going beyond their own wishes, thoughts and feelings to consider "what is going to be good for the two of us," or "what are we going to do?"

The period of engagement can be compared to the application process to a university. During engagement, a couple assesses their ability to become great lovers who are as concerned about the welfare of the other as they are about their own welfare and, through the grace of the sacrament of marriage, to surrender themselves to the welfare of their marriage and family. They are, in essence, applying for admission to marriage which is a great school of love. Like the applicant to a university, who does not know everything but has the ability to learn great things, applicants to the school of love do not know all about love, but they are open to spending a lifetime learning what it means to live "I love you."

Some engaged couples recognize that either one or both of them does not have the maturity to accept the challenge to be a great lover, and that it is inadvisable for them to marry each other. It is this ability and willingness to follow the responsible course of action, even when it hurts, that is frequently referred to as "tough love."

## I Will Love You All the Days of My Life

During this application process, couples must decide whether they will enter into a purely secular marriage. Those who are not spiritually rooted may agree to live happily for quite some time or for as long as their love lasts or by whatever other buzz phrase indicates a lack of permanency. In fact, without commitment, love is often just another four-letter word. If they choose to enter into an authentically Christian marriage, engaged couples will be expected to vow to love each other all the days of their life. Spouses who bestow the sacrament of marriage onto each other are entering into a religious life—the vowed life of marriage. The primary vow of spouses is that they *will* love each other. It is interesting that Christ does not expect a bride and groom to turn to each other to exclaim, "I love you."

During the course of a marriage enrichment session, a speaker asked couples to recall the love they had for each other on their wedding day. Not being satisfied with simply recalling the love they had on their wedding day, he asked them to actually recapture that feeling and to feel towards each other exactly as they felt on that blessed day. A couple married for about twenty years simultaneously turned to each other exclaiming, "Not on your life!"

On the one hand, they did not want to exchange the love that had developed over some twenty years for the love they had on their wedding day. They were not so much berating the love of their "novitiate" as they were treasuring the precious love fired in the crucible of twenty years of adjusting to each other, rearing children, renting apartments, moving, building a home, visiting neighbors, standing at the graveside of parents, or even of children.

They were also saying that they did not want to relive those years of learning what it meant to say, "I will love you all the days of my life." It seems that the first several (maybe fifty or so) years of marriage are committed simply to learning about marriage. In fact, it is not uncommon for spouses to say, "I am so glad he/she stuck with me during those first ten years of marriage when I did so many dumb things. Some spouses say, "I would not have given you a wooden nickel for the first twenty-five years of marriage, but these past five have made it all worthwhile." It is because it takes so long to learn about marriage that it is unfortunate that some turn their back on their commitment after only a year or so. After only a year, it is difficult to say that we have given ourself, or our spouse, love or the sacrament and its grace much of a chance.

Reflect upon the very simple phrase, "I will love you all the days of my life." This vow unites a man and a woman until they are parted by death. Considering the tenor of the times, it is a radical vow for spouses to make. In spite of the loud squeal of contradictory voices proclaiming that "no one should say yes forever" or that people change and old promises cannot be kept when conditions change," God expects spouses to commit themselves to a lifetime of loving each other.

In fact, the commitment to permanency is a vow which protects us from our impulsiveness and provides us with the ongoing opportunity to mature emotionally, spiritually and socially. The commitment to permanency does not imply a perverse thirst for pain, causing us to "hang in there." It is difficult to appreciate the joke about the Irishman who, when asked if he had ever considered divorce throughout his forty years of marriage, replied, "Divorce? Never! It is against my religion. But murder? Maybe."

Other than forgetting that murder is also against his religion, the Irishman overlooks the way in which a commitment to overcoming the tensions, problems and difficulties which are part of married life, has been a cause for deeper spiritual and emotional maturity. Most spouses are able to recall several times that they have wanted to "take a hike." However, rather than to "cop-out" they "hung in there" in a creatively tenacious effort to work out their differences and resolve their problems. They learned to cope with tension and uncertainty, tamed their impulsivity, quieted their self-interest, and become more virtuous. Their commitment to permanence has helped them mature—to become more fully human.

A young priest, who was somewhat baffled by a sincere engaged couple's insistence that he explain the meaning of commitment, asked the advice of the more experienced pastor. After the pastor explained how he could convey an understanding of commitment, the young associate and the engaged couple headed for Niagara Falls where the pastor had arranged to have a steel cable stretched across the falls and a wheelbarrow full of rocks to be placed on the one side.

With the pastor's advice firmly in mind, the associate explained that, in an effort to demonstrate commitment, he was going to push the wheelbarrow across the cable. The conscientious couple objected explaining that they cared very much for him, that they did not know who else would witness their wedding and that there was a shortage of priests. Their protestations were to no avail and the priest began to push the wheelbarrow across the cable. Although he was relatively careful as he crossed for the first time, he became more acrobatic as his confidence grew on the return trip.

When he returned to the astonished couple, he asked, "Now do you believe I can push this wheelbarrow filled with rocks to the other side and return?" Although the couple protested that they believed, it seemed that the priest intended to test them as our Lord tested Peter. Thus, he again asked if they believed. When they insisted, "Oh, yes, Rev. Father, and soon-to-be monsignor, we do believe!" However, as our Lord asked Peter three times about the depth of his love, the priest questioned the depth of the couple's belief in commitment yet a third time. They again protested: "Oh, yes, Rev. Father, soon-to-be monsignor and soon-to-be Bishop, we do believe!"

With that, the priest tipped the wheelbarrow on end, emptied the rocks, and pointing to the couple and to the wheelbarrow said, "All right, if you really believe, get in!" Through this dramatic example, the couple began to realize that commitment in marriage is saying "yes" to love when you have no guarantees about what the future holds. It requires a great deal of faith and confidence in self, other, the strength and meaning of the marital bond (like the steel cable) and the power of God's grace. In saying "yes" to love, the couple, in a sense, says "yes" to everything.

Another pastor, faced with an equally sincere couple who wondered what they could do to have a happy marriage, invited them to go to the lake with him. After sitting on the beach for a while, he asked them to walk out in the water with him so he could help them understand what they could do to have a happy marriage. When they got out more than waist deep, he held their heads under water until he dared keep them under no longer. Then, he invited the startled couple to return to the beach with him. As the couple gasped for air, the priest asked them what they had wanted more than anything else. They replied "air." The priest told them that when they wanted a good marriage as badly as they wanted air, that they would have a good marriage.

The "I will love you" in marriage commits us to love in spite of all the dumb things our spouse will reveal throughout his or her lifetime. It promises love in spite of the fact that our spouse may not know how to squeeze a tube of toothpaste, put down a toilet seat, or make a peanut butter and jelly sandwich. It promises a lifetime of loving while we reveal the full range of our stupidity, the depth of our beauty, and the scope of our wisdom.

The marriage vow promises to love when, after some ten years (or ten days) of marriage, there is a tragic automobile accident and one or the other is paralyzed or diagnosed as having an incurable disease. During engagement, the man may see his fiancée as the absolute ideal. Even her 38-24-36 is perfect. The woman sees her fiancé as perfect and especially admires his firm and sleek physique topped by a hairy chest and a full head of hair. However, in saying, "I will love you," we promise to love, when after twenty-five years of marriage, the broad mind and narrow waist have exchanged places, the hair on the chest has turned gray and the hair on the head has disappeared.

The marital vow to love promises to love even after fifty years of marriage, when one spouse cannot find his false teeth because he stepped on his glasses getting out of bed. It is edifying to attend the celebration of a fiftieth anniversary of a happily married couple. The fact that they have each other's best interests at heart is truly evident. There is no desire to take from the other. Their relationship is permeated by gentleness, tenderness and a desire to give to each other. Perhaps that pervasive feeling of love is the reward for some fifty years of loving.

It was a privilege to watch the way my wife's folks cared for each other as they passed beyond their golden anniversary. Within a few days of my father-in-law's death, my mother-in-law asked, with the deepest sense of pathos, "What can we do for him?" At that time, he could only be comforted. As she and her daughters sat by the bedside praying the Rosary, my wife noticed that she was concluding the Hail Mary by saying, "...now and at the hour of his death." Alice asked, "Mom,. have you and Dad always prayed the Hail Mary that way?" She said, "No, but now we are praying for *him*."

It is unfortunate that many seem to anticipate that they will be motivated to love by a *feeling* of love rather than by a *desire* to love. Marriage counselors, priests and others who deal with spouses in troubled marriages frequently hear the lament, "I am sorry, but I just do not feel love anymore." This lament is frequently followed by, "But I have found someone who really understands me, someone to whom I can talk, and someone for whom I *really* feel love."

This regret was expressed by a once-divorced man who had lived with a woman for six years. Now that she was thirty-five, he walked out on her so he could live with a twenty-three-year-old who, he said, had a more pleasing body which was much more firm. Unless he matures, one can predict that, once she develops some lumps and bumps, he will move on to another woman with a more firm body. This man is more lustful than loving. Although he seems capable of a genital relationship, he lacks the maturity for an emotional and spiritual relationship.

This philanderer does not seem to know that Christ did not admonish us to have warm feelings towards each other. One can guess that, as He mounted the pulpit of pulpits—the cross on Calvary, He was not overwhelmed by warm fuzzies. However, He showed us that love prompts us to give ourself up for those we love. In John 15:12, He says, "This is my commandment, love one another as I have loved you." One expects Golda is talking about a life of loving when, in *Fiddler on the Roof,* her husband Tevye asks if she loves him. She implies that it must be love because she has worked side by side with him throughout all of their marriage—washing and mending clothes, rearing children, and cooking.

Donald DeMarco theorizes about this practical statement of fact by explaining that love of itself is not a virtue. He reinforces his statements by citing the belief of St. Thomas that "love is the form of all virtues." Paul Tillich calls love "the style of life that is willed in and through each of the virtues." DeMarco reminds us that a song is not a song until it is sung; love is not love until it is channeled through a specific virtue and expressed in a specific deed. DeMarco believes that by itself, love:

> ...lacks a vehicle that connects it with reality, a direction that would give it purpose, a coordinate that would supply its meaning, a ground that would anchor its being. In order to express itself in deed, love must be combined with virtue. In its unembodied state as an idea, wish or feeling, love is not yet born and yearns to express itself in the flesh of deed. Love is brought to fulfillment by concrete action that gives it real expression.

He describes the role of virtue:

> Virtue is the capacity to transmit love into action so that love becomes embodied in deed. Love expresses itself in many ways, depending on how it can best serve man given his peculiar circumstances and his specific needs. Therefore, there must be many virtues so that no set of circumstances will prevent love from serving a human need. All virtues, then are forms through which love conveys its salutary grace. When love and virtue are separated from each other, there is neither love nor virtue.[12]

The effect of being loving might be most effectively brought home to us if we recall the times we have reached out to be loving towards someone who initially repulses us. Both St. Francis of Assisi and Ignatius of Loyola seem to be telling us this when they talk about the initial revulsion they felt towards those stricken with leprosy. It was not until he began to care for the diseased person that Francis kissed the wounds and began to feel love for the person.

C.S. Lewis, the English theological writer of essays and fiction, married when he was in his sixties. Until then, he lived as a bachelor in the world of books and ideas. He had been content to share a home with his brother and social life with male friends. Then he meet

Joy Gresham who was an American widow with whom he had corresponded for a number of years. They married in a civil ceremony, but since they only wanted to assure her right to remain in England, they continued to live in separate homes. They did not consider their marriage to be Christian until it was discovered that Mrs. Lewis had bone cancer. At that time, they both wanted to be married in the eyes of the church, the Church of England. However, rather than take his wife home to die, her pain lessened and tests showed that the cancer was arrested.

As the couple took up a rather normal domestic life, Lewis noted that what began as compassion for another human being led to something he had never considered for himself: a marriage founded on love. It was at this time that Lewis wrote his finest book, *Till We Have Faces,* a story about human and divine love. Lewis discovered the truth discovered by all authentic lovers. He came to appreciate that a marriage does not happen all at once, nor necessarily with ease. Instead, a steady stream of small decisions, showing our willingness to be attentive to the other person, wears away the sharp edges of our self-interest. The building of a life together—the making of love—it is a life long process. We learn slowly and gradually to live together, and, as this is done, as we go through thick and thin, we begin to become each other's love. We need to accept the nitty-gritty of life as part of loving. When we do this as love, rather than as drudgery, we turn the zilchy tasks into a form of love-making. The Catholic church advises newlyweds that sacrifice is difficult, but that love makes it easy and perfect love makes it a joy. How fortunate are those who are willing to love until it becomes a joy.

## Fidelity

Spouses are helped to live out their vow to love permanently through fidelity. This promise is designed to support the basic commitment to love. Unfortunately, people often think that fidelity only excludes adultery—extra-marital affairs. In reality, the commitment to fidelity goes far beyond this. The avoidance of adultery is the easiest part of the promise. Extra-marital affairs become so messy, that only a foolish, disillusioned or irresponsible and inconsiderate person would become involved in one.

Fidelity involves a willingness to give top priority—top billing—to our marriage. The person striving to live a Christ-centered life believes marriage is a vocation—a calling from God. When Christ comes first, it is inaccurate to think that one's spouse and family come second. Misunderstanding this, one fiancée complained that she wanted to be first in her future husband's life.

Although being second to Christ may not be the worst fate that could befall us, the very fact that Christ is first, places a spouse in a primary position. We need only remind ourselves that when we are plugged into Christ, we are plugged into the source of love. Thus, we are empowered to love. But if we are committed to doing the will of Christ, we will be committed to doing that which is best for our marriage and family life. Christ-centered persons realize that they receive strength only when they give it. In the natural order, we have to hold onto strength to maintain it. But in the divine order, we only receive when we give. As we pour out more and more intelligence and energy, God gives us the strength we need. This brings about a great transformation in the soul of the Christ-centered person who becomes a captive of Christ's love.

The woman who did not understand what it means for Christ to be first in the life of her fiancé needs to realize that there is a small piece cut out of the top of every human heart. Some say this symbolizes the piece that was torn out of the universal heart of humans at the time of the crucifixion of Christ. It is an Irish folk tradition that God kept a little piece of our heart for Himself. He then sent us into the world to try to fill up our hearts with all of the love we could. We will never be totally happy, totally in love and totally able to love someone with a full heart. Our heart will never be truly filled with love until it returns to God to recover the little piece of our heart waiting for us for all eternity.

Fidelity in marriage implies that the welfare of our marriage and family life comes before friends, family of origin, recreation, civic duty, church involvement and work. There should not be a conflict between fidelity to marriage and family life and the other commitments in our life. Unfortunately, spouses often find themselves having to choose between the welfare of their marriage and family life and the need for recognition in their public lives. While there are a variety of reasons for this, one important reason may be that those with whom we are involved daily may not be equally committed to living a Christ-centered life. Thus, family commitments are diminished.

The seductive wiles of a tempter or temptress to an extra-marital affair may pale into insignificance compared to the temptations of friends who want us to play golf, softball, go to a football or hockey game, or go hunting. The same may be true for the lure of recognition in our community, social groups or church. Professional and occupational recognition steers many from a course of marital fidelity.

One of the unfortunate dilemmas experienced by spouses is that they may frequently feel they will ultimately help their marriage by a "little bit of infidelity." They may think that the money earned through extra work, nuturing a particular friendship or involvement in a particular social group may briefly compromise fidelity, but that there will be long-term benefit to the marriage. Unfortunately, many spouses, who cave into this temptation, seem to compromise themselves right out of marriage. There are many who work to accumulate material conveniences and all that would make it look like they have many pieces of the good life. Unfortunately, they may lose their marriage in the process.

We are familiar with the era in which a husband worked to provide the good life and to climb the ladder of success. However, as he grew further and further away from his spouse, she became increasingly disillusioned. When such a man stopped to take a breath, and looked back, he found his wife had drifted far beyond his reach. Although he may have been grief-stricken, he may have had to admit that he was helpless to repair the damaged relationship. We may have entered upon a time in which there is a slight variation of this theme. Now some women who have made a primary commitment to career are stopping to take a breath, looking back and realizing that they have lost that which they had taken for granted.

One wonders about the effect of commercials depicting modern women as unequaled champions in the "triatholon." The contemporary woman is portrayed as being at the top of the corporate ladder, a well-groomed, trim and accomplished athlete, impeccable homemaker, sultry wife, and all purpose mother and/or grandmother. In an earlier era, the "triatholon" event was confined to the home where she was expected to be an economist in the kitchen, a hussy in the bedroom and a lady in the parlor. Of course, some expressed their hostility about these expectations by being ladies in the kitchen, hussies in the parlor and economists in the bedroom.

## Love That Gives Life

In an effort to support the desire of spouses to permanently live out the promise to love, the church also urges them to promise to be open to the opportunity to cooperate with God in the act of co-creation. Again, this expectation stands in opposition to the values of the larger society which caught in the strangle-hold of selfishness, wages chemical, surgical, and mechanical warfare against fertility. Society permits and even encourages aborting those children who have somehow sallied around the contraceptive efforts and managed to be conceived.

Because of her all-consuming desire to help us live out the wishes of Christ, the church guided by the Holy Spirit has understood that love is more than just a hunger to be fulfilled by developing a oneness with a spouse. It is also the making of a home and family. Gerlad Vann recognized this when we wrote in a 1956 pamphlet, entitled *Christian Married Love,* that when love is turned upon itself we rob it of its natural fulfillment and we take its heart and life. This commitment to fecundity recognizes how hard it is for us to stop being self-centered. Love is self-diffusive. Its whole nature is to be outward-turning, to express itself in something, as the instinct of every artist is to express the thing he sees and loves. Human love is complete and perfected when the image of the Blessed Trinity is fulfilled in it. This fulfillment is most powerfully seen when the couple's love becomes a third reality—a child.

Like the commitment to permanency and fidelity, a willingness to cooperate with each other and God to create a new life is considered so fundamental to marriage that if each of the spouses cannot make this commitment, a priest would not witness the marriage. If it was found that one of the parties only spoke the words, but had no intention of keeping the promise, the marriage would be considered invalid. The church is saying that permanency, fidelity and an openness to new life are absolutely integral to Christian marriage.

Although the child is the fruit of the love and unity of the parents, the loving unity is made perfect through the making of the family—the bearing and upbringing of the child. It is that common task, above all, that makes men and women unselfish lovers. Parenthood provides an opportunity to learn a wisdom, a patience, a common understanding and a common joy that it would be difficult to learn elsewhere.

As one considers the realities related to the value and effect of children, it is important to think about those couples who, because of agonizing infertility problems, are unable to conceive children. Since they desire children, their marriage is valid. The church does not teach that married persons have to have children. She teaches that receptivity to new life is fundamental to marriage. There is a positive responsibility to procreate unless there are very serious reasons to the contrary. Unfortunately, there are couples who because of physical problems are unable to conceive and bear children.

Loving couples, faced with the painful reality of fertility problems, are challenged to guard against the tendency for their love for each other to only consume itself. They must go outside themselves to serve others. Like the celibate, they must have spiritual children for whom they care and to whom they give themselves. Many of these couples make enormous contributions to parishes, schools and a variety of volunteer programs.

The importance of loving beyond ourselves is conveyed by a missionary who hired a Tibetan guide to take him over the Himalayas. They had gone up a short distance when the weather took a sudden turn for the worse. It was not long before they realized they were in serious trouble. As they sat and tried to regain their energy, they overheard a man groaning in the snow. The missionary said, "I think I hear someone groaning in the abyss."

The Tibetan asked, "What difference does it make? We're almost dead ourselves." However, the missionary went over to find the man, and finding him, he assisted him. This act so revived his own energies that he was again able to travel. After taking the stricken man to another village he returned to find the Tibetan guide frozen to death on the ice. God's grace will re-energize and inflame our hearts so that we need not be left freezing on the ice.

## Responding to God's Gift

We are surrounded with many signs of God's love. Yet as we look at polluted streams, lakes and rivers, or scarred countryside and at littered parks, we wonder about the quality of our response to God's love. As we are reminded of excesses such as overeating, smoking and alcohol, we must wonder if we have been any less willing to pollute the gift of our bodies than we have been to pollute our natural resources. We are reminded of the many people who pollute their bodies with the contraceptive pill, or in other ways wage war against their fertility, we wonder about our basic attitude towards God's gift of life. Abortion seems to serve notice on God that He can take and "stuff" His most basic gift, His most fundamental natural resource.

As we recognize some of the ways in which the signs of God's love are disregarded or rejected, we wonder about the extent to which we become careless about God's gift of marital love. This gift, which requires massive doses of tender loving care, is like a diamond, which at one point was only a glob of carbon. Then, as it stuck tenaciously to its job, it became a diamond—a jewel. Spouses need to assess the extent to which they are tenderly nurturing their love and engaged couples need to explore the depth of their commitment to a life of cultivating the gift of love they will receive through the sacrament of marriage.

Avoid fitting the stereotype of the couple glued to their TV screen with one lamenting, "If you can't be happy with cable TV, what will make you happy!?" Equally as bad is the picture of the couple at the breakfast table looking indifferent to the way they appear to each other. The husband's attention may be glued to the newspaper while the attention of his wife is riveted to the TV set. Another stereotype is that of the spouses whose backs are turned to each other signalling their total turn-off of each other.

We care for the gift of marital love by reminding ourselves of Christ's admonition to build our home upon rock—the word of God and not upon sand—the ways of the world (Matt. 7:24-27). This plan, given by the master builder, is implemented in a multitude of ways as spouses go about the day-to-day business of living out their vow to love. Paul's practical advice to the Corinthians (1 Cor. 13:4-7) helps us understand that we are to seek to complement each other rather than to be jealous of the other's talents, interests and activitics. We are to be patient and kind as we spend a life-time adapting and adjusting to each other's peculiarities and idiosyncrasies.

We need to be patient when one or the other is sick, whether that is something as minor as a cold or hayfever or a tragic illness. Many of us can be lovingly patient and understanding for about twelve hours. Then, we seem to begin demanding immediate recovery. The rather terse question, "Can't you do something about that?" may not be beneficial. We are reminded to put aside haughtiness, selfishness and rudeness and to be tender, kind and gentle towards each other. Rather than to "fight" for his or her own way, the loving spouse seeks that which is best for the welfare of the marriage.

Rather than to justify our bad moods with the all too glib comment that, "I am in a bad mood and you will just have to stay away from me this year," we are challenged to not be irritable and touchy. Rather than to be the gunnysacker looking for grievances to shelf, the loving spouse is willing to forgive and to seek reconciliation and healing (Col. 4:12-13).

Of course, since they recognize the importance of being reconciled with each other, they will also recognize the importance of being reconciled with God. They will know that the sin in our life separates us from God. In separating us from God, those faults cause some static in our relationship with God. This faulty connection interferes with our ability to be loving. Thus, in their ongoing effort to live a life of love, spouses will recognize the importance of the sacrament of reconciliation. It will be helpful for any person who is affiliated with a denomination which recognizes the sacrament of reconciliation (John 21:21-23) to enter fully into the reception of this sacrament as part of the preparation for marriage. Penance and reconciliation are some of the steps one takes as part of the entrance into a life of loving.

Beyond an openness to forgiveness and reconciliation, loving spouses are willing to let little things "go by the board." Spouses whose lifetime building project is guided by Paul's plan, will never rejoice in what is wrong by playing "I gottcha." This is a game played by those who rejoice in being done onto. In this way, they are able to shout "foul", back the other into the corner, and walk off the penalty while self-righteously announcing the infraction to the larger world. In building their marriage, they should be guided by Paul's advice to the Galatians (5:13-14) that we are to serve one another.

Loving spouses will build their home materially, emotionally and spiritually. They rent an apartment, build a house, beg, borrow and buy used, unfinished and new furniture, hang pictures, plant flowers, lay sod and do a thousand and one things to turn a house into a home. They will recognize that they express and grow in love by working together on the life-building tasks like doing dishes, cleaning the home, going off to work, and preparing meals. The couple building on rock will have an integrated view of God's gift of sex. Although they will recognize its importance, they will not exaggerate the role of sex. If they are blessed with a pregnancy, they will rejoice in and care for the unborn life growing within the womb of the mother. On the day of the birth, they will thank God for this living sign of the love between them.

The couple blessed with children quickly realizes that the gift of their marital love cannot be turned in on themselves. Instead, the radiant glow from that love begins to nourish and to enrich the lives of others. As their love is serving others, they become increasingly aware that they must build their home upon a solid foundation. They may have less time with each other as increasing demands are made upon them by children, grandparents, aging parents, work, community and church reponsibilities.

Spouses will grow in and show their love for each other by being willing to waste some time together, to grow old together and to watch the living signs of their love in this, the next, and even the next generation beyond their own. They will discover a new need to be patient and understanding as they grow older and may not hear each other so well, as they have trouble writing notes large enough for the other to read, and as they cannot quite keep up with the other when they go out for a walk.

As spouses commit themselves to a lifetime of loving, they will become more closely identified with the magnificent love of Christ. Spouses learn that love demands selflessness over selfishness. They find that geniune love does not seek its own pleasure and satisfaction from the other, but always the good of the other.

Our capacity to be as concerned about the welfare of the other as we are about our own welfare over a lifetime together transforms us into magnificent lovers who, like Christ, are able to give up ourselves for the one we love. For the one who truly loves, it is always the beloved who counts. Emeric Lawrence states that the chief characteristic of true love is respect for the personality of the beloved. He cites Monsignor Guardini's comment that geniune love, springing from reverence for the personality of the other, is like the sun shining on a grain of wheat burning in the ground. As the sun's rays shine on and warm the seed and help to release the inner power in the seed to bring growth, so does genuine love release love so that the beloved freely gives himself or herself back to the lover. This kind of love is the most precious possession in the world of the married couple. It is the one thing necessary in their lives. Christ in the sacrament of marriage helps spouses reach toward such an unselfish love.

The Greek distinctions between Eros, Filia and Agape distinguishes types of love. The Eros type of love is frequently directed towards self-realization. The Filia type of love refers to a love for humanity. This is represented in the name of the city of Philadelphia as the city of brotherly love. Filia love is irrespective of class, race, sexuality or other distinction. It too conveys a feeling deeper than liking—a loving. Liking resides in the emotions, but loving rests in the will. Since emotions can change, the object of our likes or dislikes can also change. Thus, liking is whimsical. Feeling is in the will and love is subject to the command of the will. Some

*CHAPTER 14*

# The Challenge of Marriage

No matter how long we are married and no matter how nice it can be, we never really get it all together. For instance, one partner may think that it is absolutely beautiful if they can be in bed by about 10:00 p.m. One of the spouses may think that they should be "up and at em" by about 4:00 a.m. These spouses will be sources of tension to each other if one has been known to sleep until the ghastly late hour of 7:00 a.m. There are those who sleep out of sheer necessity and others who sleep for recreation. While one reminds the other that *idleness* is the devil's workshop, the sleeper may proclaim that *busyness* is the devil's workshop.

In fact, these differences are like the grains of sand used to make sandpaper. During the courtship and initial years of marriage, the grains may be relatively coarse. This coarseness rubs away the rough edges, gouges and high spots so that the couple is able to bring about a fit—a oneness. After some years of adaptation and adjustment, they may find they are fitting rather well. Once that basic fit is achieved, the differences have the effect of fine sandpaper which, rather than to sand, tends more to polish and to bring out the beauty of wood. This continual polishing brings out the beauty and depth (the real humanness) of the spouses. If a couple is going to adapt and adjust to their differences, they will be called upon to become people of virtue. Deriving from the Latin *vir,* virtue means strength which implies beauty. Christian people of virtue have accepted the challenge to become more Christ-like or to "be perfect as our Heavenly Father is perfect."

If we are going to adjust to the "dumb things" that are done by our spouse and to the traumas presented to us in marriage, we must become people of virtue. In so many instances, we distort the richness of our humanity by excusing our mistakes with the simplistic rationalization, "Well, you know, I am only human." Being under the deluded notion that imperfections prove their humanity, some persons seem to brag about their mistakes. In reality, we are called upon to recognize that we are created in God's image and likeness. We are most human when we accurately reflect the image of the God in whom we have been created. This image is accurately reflected as we become people of deep and penetrating virtue.

Great patience, tenderness, gentleness and understanding is required if spouses are going to deal effectively with the "dumb" (different) things done by the other. Great prudence will be required if they are going to work together to make effective decisions about the establishment of their priorities and the way in which their lives are going to be lived. A deep sense of justice is required for spouses who are faced with distinguishing between a right and wrong course of action. An internalized sense of justice will help them decide which one should give in on a particular issue on which they are deadlocked. Spouses will need, in cooperation with God's grace, to develop the virtue of temperance. This will be helpful in their effort to make appropriate use of God's various gifts. Of course, fortitude is absolutely essential if spouses are going to be able to "stick with each other." Nevertheless, there will be instances and periods of discouragement and perhaps, even desperation. It is during those times when they will be tempted to "take a hike" that it will be essential to have the ability to "hang in there" while they ride out the storm.

Of course, the virtue of love supports and permeates all virtues. "Love is the one thing that cannot hurt your neighbor; that is why it is the source of every one of the commandments (Romans 13:10)." Paul becomes more detailed about this when he explains:

> If I speak with human tongues and angelic as well, but do not have love, I am a noisy gong, a clanging cymbal. If I have the gift of prophecy and, with full knowledge, comprehend all mysteries, if I have faith great enough to move mountains, but have not love, I am nothing. If I give everything I have to feed the poor and hand over my body to be burned, but have not love, I gain nothing.
>
> Love is patient; love is kind. Love is not jealous, it does not put on airs, it is not snobbish. Love is never rude, it is not self-seeking, it is not prone to anger; neither does it brood over injuries. Love does not rejoice in what is wrong but rejoices with the truth. There is no limit to love's forbearance, to its trust, its hope, its power to endure.
>
> Love never fails. Prophecies will cease, tongues will be silent, knowledge will pass away. Our knowledge is imperfect and our prophesying is imperfect. When the perfect comes, the imperfect will pass away. When I was a child, I used to talk like a child, think like a child, reason like a child. When I became a man, I put childish ways aside. Now we see distinctly, as in a mirror; then we shall see face to face. My knowledge is imperfect now; then I shall know even as I am known. There are in the end three things that last: faith, hope, and love, and the greatest of these is love (I Cor. 13:1-13).

If couples appreciate the importance of marrying someone who will help them get to heaven, they will see how important it is for each of them to direct their attention to Jesus. As each spouse seeks to be more like Christ, the couple will find that they are becoming more alike. The task of marriage is not much different than the plan to create a beautiful piece of furniture.

First, a basic plan and design must be followed. The plan for marriage has been given to us by God as He reveals Himself through holy scripture, sacred tradition and through the teachings of the church. Then, the pieces must be cut and made to fit. After they are sanded and drawn together, a craftsman must patiently chisel, plane and sand to create a perfect fit. After this, there is the rather tedious and painstaking process of sanding, polishing and finishing. In the initial stages, the craftsman takes out the rough spots and draws the pieces together. However, as the finishing process continues, the craftsman is not so much eliminating imperfections as he is drawing out the beauty, depth and richness of the wood.

This is exactly what happens in marriage. The spouses spend some years developing the virtues that will allow them to be drawn together as one. As the years go by, as this fit becomes more comfortable and as they become more virtuous, that is more Christ-like, one begins to see the real beauty of their humanity. After all, they are only becoming what they were intended to be—images of God.

Whenever our behavior in elementary school fell short of the teacher's expectations, we were called to the front of the room where we had to stand facing the other students with our hands held out—palms up. The teacher would strike our hands with a ruler, pointer or switch. This continued until we showed some sign of contrition. What really griped me was that, if the teacher broke the ruler, we had to pay for a new ruler. I also had great difficulty understanding why we were expected to be thankful for the thrashing. The explanation was that we were being helped to become perfect as our Heavenly Father was perfect. That did not mean much to a mere third or fourth grader who, at night would pray, "Dear God, if You do not want to make me a better boy, it is quite all right. I am having a good time the way that it is."

However, some years later, I began to appreciate the importance of becoming what we are meant to become—perfect as the Heavenly Father is perfect. Spouses help each other achieve this perfection by expecting to spend a lifetime adapting and adjusting to one another. Thus, the "horrible irritations" of life—messy toothpaste tubes, spinach with no hollandaise sauce, and cars with empty gas tanks end up becoming sources of our sanctification. It seems that almost unintentionally, we help each other to become saints. Of course, the basic purpose of life is to become saints—to join God in His Kingdom. As family, friends and relatives gather to celebrate a couple's golden anniversary, they may comment, "My goodness, they even look alike." After they have spent a lifetime adapting and adjusting to each other, they will come face-to-face with God, who will look at them and say, "You look exactly like my Son, please come and spend eternity with us."

# *For Further Reading*

## General

Bryson, Jeff and Rebecca, eds. *Dual-Career Couples.* New York: Human Sciences Press, 1978. 120 pp. $9.95.

The authors cite a government survey indicating that nearly fifty percent of all married women are currently employed. The contributors to the book explore the effects of this situation on child rearing and marital happiness. The address is 72 5th Ave., New York, N.Y. 10011.

Evoy, John J. and Maureen O'Keefe. *The Man and the Woman: Psychology of Human Love.* New York: Sheed and Ward, 1968. 143 pp. $5.00.

Provides a deeper understanding of the basic human relationship of love.

Ford, Edward E. and Steven Englund. *Permanent Love: Practical Steps to a Lasting Relationship.* Minneapolis: Winston Press, Inc., 1979.

The authors explain that there is no easy path to love anymore than there is an easy path through life. The comparison is apt, for loving is essentially an expression of daily living, not the dreamy-eyed creation of romance foisted on Western society in the late 11th Century by bards and troubadours. The authors intend to offer a calm, reasonable antidote to the ravages and caricatures of romantic love in our culture. The address is 430 Oak Grove, Minneapolis, MN 55403.

Frankl, Viktor E. *Man's Search for Meaning: An Introduction to Logotherapy.* New York: Washington Square Press, 1959.

A classic book written after the author's release from a Nazi concentration camp. It shows how, in spite of desperate circumstances, he continued to see meaning in life.

Hitchcock, James. *What is Secular Humanism?* Ann Arbor, Mich.: Servant Books, 1982. 158 pp.$6.95.

Probes the origins of secular humanism, its impact on Western civilization and its probable future course.

Lederer, William J. and Don D. Jackson. *The Mirages of Marriage.* New York: W.W. Norton and Co., Inc. 1968. 473 pp. $7.95.

A classic and incisive analysis of marriage. The authors present a systems concept in dealing with the realities of marriage.

Martlet, Gustave. "Christological Theses on the Sacrament of Marriage." *Origins.* Vol. 8, p. 200.

Newcomb, Paul R. "Cohabitation in America: An Assessment of Consequences." *Journal of Marriage and the Family.* Vol. 41, No. 3 (August 1979), pp. 597-603.

A survey of empirical research with regard to cohabitation. The major consequences of cohabitation, both pro and con, are identified for five groups. A number of references are listed.

*Our Family.* Battleford, Sask., Canada.

This is an excellent family magazine providing helpful ideas for living Christian marriage.A gift subscription would be appropriate for a shower or wedding gift. The address is Box 249, Battleford, Sask. Canada, SOM-OEO.

Peck, Scott. *The Road Less Traveled.* New York: Simon and Schuster, 1979. 316 pp.

The author insists that there is no distinction between the process of achieving spiritual growth and achieving mental health. This process of achieving spiritual growth is based on love. Along with five aspects of what he believes constitutes true love, he concludes that love is an act of the will, not a feeling. He says love is "...the will to extend one's self for the purpose of nuturing one's own or another's spiritual growth."

Quesnell, Jack G. *Marriage: A Discovery Together.* Notre Dame, Ind.: Sexton Printing, 1974. 262 pp. $8.95

The author shows that whatever form and style a marriage relationship may take, the spouses must have an awareness of themselves and an understanding of their own as well as each other's needs. He shows how these needs can be met, how self-inflicted hazards can be avoided and how a creative relationship can be developed.

conversion and the outcome of interfaith marriages. The address is 1312 Massachusetts Ave. N.W., Washington, D.C., 20005.

Larsson, Clotye M., ed. *Marriage Across the Color Line.* Chicago: Johnson Publishing Co., 1965. 294 pp. $4.95.

Through documentary accounts, the reader is able to feel the "slings and arrows" to which partners in racially-mixed marriages are subjected. The reader feels the "stare" which so many intermarried couples report.

National Conference of Catholic Bishops: *Statement on the Implementation of the Apostolic Letter on Mixed Marriages,* Jan. 1, 1971. 15 pp.

Paul VI. *An Apostolic Letter Issued "Motu Proprio" Determining Norms for Mixed Marriages,* Mar. 31, 1970. 7 pp.

"The Sanctity of Marriage." *Origins.* Vol. 8, No. 28 (Dec. 28, 1978), pp. 446-447.

A statement issued by the Eastern-Orthodox Roman Catholic consultation in the United States.

Schiappa, Barbara D. *Mixing: Catholic-Protestant Marriages in the 1980's.* New York: Paulist Press, 1982. 143 pp. $5.95.

Practical steps for working through the differences experienced in interfaith marriages.

Toon, Peter. *Protestants and Catholics.* Ann Arbor, Mich.: Servant Books, 1983. 160 pp. $5.95.

This book is a guide to understanding the differences among Christians. It deals with issues such as how and why the Protestant Reformation developed, what Catholics and Protestants teach about the Bible, how they look at authority, what they teach about the Sacraments and what Catholics believe about Mary.

Whalen, William J. *Separated Brethren.* Huntington, Ind.: Our Sunday Visitor. 1974.

A survey of the 1970's, which remains relevant, of Protestant, Anglican, Orthodox, Old Catholic, Jewish, Buddhist and other denominations and cults in the United States. The author cites the statement of the Decrees on Ecumenism of the Second Vatican Council advising that Catholics must get to know the outlook of separated brethren. The address is Noll Plaza, Huntington, ID 46750.

## Money Management, Insurance and Home Buying

Blodgett, Richard E. *The New York Times Book of Money.* New York: Quadrangle/The New York Times Co., Inc., 1979. New and Rev. 223 pp. $6.95.

Contains information about every major area of money management.

Bowman, George M. *How to Succeed with Your Money.* Chicago.: The Moody Bible Institute, 1960, 1974. 191 pp. $1.50.

Published monthly at 10880 Wilshire Blvd., Los Angeles, CA 90024.

Money Management Institute. *Money Management—Your Savings and Investment Dollar; Money Management—Managing Your Credit;* and *Money Management—Your Financial Plan..* Prospect Heights, Ill.: Household Finance Corporation, 1973.

Other educational material regarding finances is available. Write for a complete list to 2700 Sanders Road, Prospect Heights, Ill 60070.

Phalon, Richard. *Your Money: How to Make It Work Harder Than You Do..* New York: St. Martin Press, Inc., 1979. 317 pp. $8.95.

This strategy book is a how-to guide to personal finance and money management for consumers whose resources don't require professional management. The author stresses your money plan, borrowing effectively, insurance, financing the right home, getting more interest, investments, and much more.

Quinn, Jane Bryant. *Everyone's Money Book.* New York: Delacorte Press, 1979. 868 pp. $14.95 hardbound. $9.95 paperback.

Easy to read, easy to understand advice on savings, spending, earning, lending, borrowing, insuring, moving, investing, budgeting, consumer rights, taxes and future security. This was very helpful in preparing Chapter 9.

Spielman, Peter and Aaron Zelman with Dean Sharp. *The Life Insurance Conspiracy Made Elementary by Sherlock Holmes.*

New York: Simon and Schuster, 1976, 1979. 171 pp. $4.95 paperback.

This book stresses that the key to avoid being "taken in" is to know how to buy life insurance rather than having it sold to you. It contains an excellent financial planning kit to analyze your insurance needs.

VanCaspel, Venita. *Money Dynamics for the 1980's.* Reston, Va.: Reston Publishing Co., Inc., 1980. 718 pp. $15.00.

VanCaspel, Venita. *The Power of Money Dynamics.* Reston, Va.: Reston Publishing Co., Inc. 1983. 661 pp. $18.00.

These two books, written by a professional financial planner, offer up-to-date information on investing, home buying, life insurance—the great national consumer dilemma, lending your dollars, planning for later years and taking a financial inventory. An excellent appendix with tables on compounding interest, comparing interest, comparing interest rates and cost of investing. This book was especially helpful in preparing the content of chapter 9.

Young, Amy Ross. *It Only Hurts Between Paydays.* Denver, Co.: B/P Publications, Inc., Accent Books, 1975. 128 pp. $1.95.

A practical and exciting plan for getting control of your personal finances. Easy to read. For those already in financial trouble, the book offers steps to start on the road to recovery.

## Sex, and Family Planning

Aguilar, Nona. *No-Pill, No-Risk Birth Control.* New York: Rawson, Wade Publishers, Inc., 1980. 254 pp. $6.95.

A book for those worried about artificial birth control methods which are sometimes dangerous and often interruptive. This book outlines a hazard free, effective method that relies solely on a woman's own body signals.

Ball, John and Nancy. *Joy in Human Sexuality.* Collegeville, Minn.: The Liturgical Press, 1975. 65 pp. $ .95.

A gem of a book which helps women gain a better understanding of themselves and men gain a better understanding of women.

Bertocci, Peter, *Sex, Love, and the Person.* New York: Sheed and Ward, Inc., 1967.

Christenson, Larry and Nordis. *The Christian Couple.* Minneapolis: Bethany Fellowship, Inc., 1977. 186 pp. $5.95.

A Lutheran pastor and his wife who write in support of Natural Family Planning and of how they came from contraception to NFP and what it means to them.

DeMarco, Donald. "World Population—Voices of Reason." *Our Family.* April 1979, pp. 10-14.

A helpful article summarizing and critiquing many of the arguments used by those claiming the world is over-populated. It may be helpful to those who do not necessarily favor contraception, but believe population pressures demand drastic measures.

Derrick, Christopher. *Sex and Sacredness.* San Francisco: Ignatius Press, 1982. 219 pp. $10.00.

The author intends to promote understanding between Catholic morality and the "permissive society."

de Vinck, Jose. *The Virtue of Sex.* New York: Hawthorn Books, 1966, 255 pp. $4.95.

The author maintains that all is from God and that the theology of sex must begin with the inner reality of the person of Christ. The address is 70 - 5th Ave., New York. N.Y. 10011.

Finnis, John. *Natural Law and Natural Rights.* Oxford: Clarendon, 1980. 425 pp. $19.95.

Considered by many to be the most significant work on the natural law to appear in modern times. It is, along with John Paul II's works, a reminder that we left Thomism at our own peril, at the point of not understanding what we are about without it, even within Western intellectual tradition itself.

Ernst, Siefried. *Man, the Greatest of Miracles: An Answer to the Sexual Counter-evolution.* Collegeville, Minn: The Liturgical Press, 1976. 172 pp. $3.95.

Ford, John C. and Germain Grisez. "Contraception and the Infallibility of the Magisterum." *Theological Studies,* June 1978.

This article seeks to demonstrate that *Humanae Vitae* meets the conditions for an infallible exercise of the ordinary magisterium set forth by Vatican II.

Grisez, Germain and Russell Shaw. *Beyond the New Morality: The Responsibilities of Freedom.* Notre Dame: University of Notre Dame Press, 1974. 220 pp. $3.25.

The authors use numerous examples of real life ethical problems and responses to them in a successful effort to discuss ethics in a manner which is non-technical and easy to understand.

Hogan, Richard M., *The Wonder of Human Sexuality.* St. Paul: The Leaflet Missal Co., 1985. 71 pp.

A booklet intended for both parents and teenagers which places human sexuality in the context of our creation in the image of God. The address is 419 W. Minnehaha Ave., St. Paul, MN 55103.

Hogan, Richard M., and John M. LeVoir. *Covenant of Love.* Garden City, N.Y.: Doubleday and Co., Inc., 1985. 246 pp. $15.95.

In conveying the central message of the pontificate of John Paul II, the authors explore the influence of Christ on the modern family, human intimacy, and sexuality. They illustrate the Holy Father's response to materialism, sterilization, premarital sex, abortion, polygamy, adultery, and lust, contraception and artificial conception and homosexuality.

*The International Journal of Natural Family Planning,* Collegeville, Minn.: St. John's University.

An excellent quarterly which contains numerous articles related to the material discussed in these chapters. The address is Collegeville, MN 56321.

John Paul II. "Stand Up for Human Life." *Origins.* Vol. 9, No. 18 (October 18, 1979), pp. 277-80.

Text of the Holy Father's homily regarding marriage which was delivered in Washington, D.C. He states that Christian marriage must be inspired by the Gospel and thus be open to life. He explains that joyful family life "requires much from both the parents and the children. Each member of the family has to become in a special way, the servant of the others and share the burdens."

Joyce, Mary Rosera. *How Can a Man and Woman Be Friends?* Collegeville, Minn.: St. John's University Press, n.d.

The address is Collegeville, MN 56321.

Kelly, George A. *The Battle For the American Church.* Chapter VI, "The Birth Control Battle," Garden City, N.Y.: Doubleday and Co., 1979, pp. 127-98.

While describing the various means of family planning, the author explains that the secular world has not provided an effective answer to the family planning dilemma.

Quesnell, Jack G. *Three to Get Ready: A Guide For the Engaged*, Collegeville, Minn.: The Liturgical Press, 1976. 156 pp. $3.50.

Chapters 11-17 contain a very interesting description of the Cycle of Devolution which refers to the way in which a permissive approach to sex has served to rob sex of its meaning.

Roberts, H.J. *Is Vasectomy Safe?* West Palm Beach, Fla,: Sunshine Academic Press, 1979. 289 pp.

Dr. Roberts does not consider Catholic morality in supporting the notion that vasectomies are an "Iatrogenic Illness"—physican induced. The address is 304 27th St., West Palm Beach, FL 33407.

Seaman, Barbara and Gideon. *Women and the Crisis in Sex Hormones*. New York: Rossen and Associates, Inc., 1977. 502 pp. $12.95.

A readable and authoritative consideration of birth control, of interest not only to women, but also to men. The authors document the dangers of hormones.

Von Hildebrand, Dietrich. *The Encyclical Humanae Vitae: A Sign of Contradiction*. Chicago, Ill.: Franciscan Herald Press, 1969.

Von Hildebrand, Dietrich. *In Defense of Purity*. Chicago: Franciscan Herald Press, 1970. $2.50.

This book, printed originally in 1930, provides a classic study of human love. It is an analysis of the Catholic ideals of purity and virginity.

Wojtyla, Karol. *Fruitful and Responsible Love.* New York: The Seabury Press, 1979. 74 pp. $.95.

While a Cardinal, John Paul II wrote on the role and purpose of sexuality and marriage. The comments were written ten years after *Humanae Vitae* and served as the theological and pastoral foundation for ensuing ecumenical dialogue. The volume also contains reactions by some of the distinguished Catholic and non-Catholic participants.

## ABOUT THE AUTHOR

Jack and his wife, Alice, have lived in Minnesota for most of Jack's professional life. They have been very actively involved at the St. Paul Catholic Youth Center for most of their married life. Jack is engaged in the private practice of Marriage and Family Therapy and is also recognized as a prominent author and lecturer. He received his B.A. degree from Saint John's University and his Master's degree in Social Work and Certificate in Marriage Therapy from the University of Minnesota. His writings, audio, and video programs reflect his more than a quarter century of active, innovative, and excitingly rich experience of serving as a marriage and family therapist and a seminar and conference leader for teens, the engaged, spouses and parents. His ability to conduct retreats, conferences, and seminars in Pastoral and Marriage and Family Therapy has led to high praise from those best qualified to judge—those who have participated in the programs he has offered.

*Other Materials by*
*Jack Quesnell*

## MARRIAGE AS A RELIGIOUS LIFE

Four 30 minute audio-cassettes, $29.95

In this audio-cassette series, Jack explores marriage as a vowed religious life. Spouses are challenged to commit themselves to living a life of love. This helps us to become good, holy and virtuous people. Jack shares approaches for building a relationship and living out the purpose of marriage—to help each other get to Heaven.

## THE MESSAGE OF CHRIST AND THE COUNSELOR

This book has been enormously popular with and helpful to Christian psychotherapists, Emergency Pregnancy Service Counselors as well as to parents and spouses. A mother of teenagers thought the subtitle should be, "A GUide for Parents of Teenagers." Jack believes that it is important to clearly enunciate a value system. ($2.00)

## MARRIAGE: A DISCOVERY TOGETHER

This always popular book of Jack's explains that whatever form a marriage relationship may take, it involves two people and Christ. Spouses are invited to develop an awareness of themselves and an understanding of the other. ($8.95)

## HOLY TERRORS AND HOLY PARENTS

Jack approaches parenting in his typically helpful and direct manner. He synthesizes sound psychological principles with practical Christian values, and clearly points out how the principles are to be implemented. The book is a source of knowledge, inspiration and comfort for Christian parents. ($6.95)

*Send Order to:*

ALICE QUESNELL
3429 Stinson Blvd.
Minneapolis, MN 55418
(612) 789-1393